The Gospel of Thomas

A Blueprint for Spiritual Growth

By David F. Capps

The Gospel of Thomas,
A Blueprint for Spiritual Growth

2005 First Printing

For information regarding permission to reprint material from this book, please mail or FAX your request in writing to The Gnostic Wisdom Foundation at the address below, or go to our website at www.gnosticwisdom.org and leave an e-mail at cs@gnosticwisdom.org.

ISBN 0-9774198-0-0

Published by:
The Gnostic Wisdom Foundation
HC-11 Box 366
Kamiah, ID 83536
866-389-5233
FAX 208-926-4169

www.gnosticwisdom.org

Cover design by Connection Graphics Inc.

Printed in U.S.A.

Acknowledgements

This book would not have been possible without the loving support and faith of my dear wife and life partner, Miriam G. Carroll. This book is also the result of teaching presented in our spiritual growth class, the students of which are an inspiration to me in their faithful attention to spiritual principles, their curiosity and their openness to learn new facts and details of our religious and spiritual past. I would also like to acknowledge Carol Asher, Miriam G. Carroll, Rhonda Carroll and Julie Igo for their help in reading and refining the information in this book.

Thank you and God bless you.

David F. Capps

Table of Contents

About the Author

David began his spiritual quest in 1970 at the age of 23. He had become disenchanted with the Christian approach to religion and embarked on a study of Eastern religions. David's quest, like that of so many other people, was really a search for truth. The vast array of information available quickly leaves the searcher dazed and confused, hoping to find something which "feels right" and "makes sense". David spent several months considering what the truth might look like so it could be recognized when it was seen. He decided the truth was something which remained largely unchanged by the passage of time, the effect of different cultures, and the great distances separating the people and religious systems around the globe. By comparing spiritual principles from different religious systems and sorting out the differences, a core set of basic "truths" emerged. This allowed a focusing of effort on a simple set of spiritual principles and practices.

This focused practice resulted in his having a classical mystical experience in February of 1985, where David found himself standing in the presence of God. Everything physical had disappeared. Only he and God remained. During this time David experienced the overwhelming unconditional love which comes from God. The revelations regarding life, death and the true nature of spirit quickly followed. The intensity of this experience slowly faded over a three month period. By early summer he was asking, "Is this it? You bring me into Your presence and Your light and in three months it fades and goes away?" He was shown that if he continued with the spiritual practices he had learned he would permanently re-enter this state of grace he experienced during his mystical experience. That took place seven years later, in 1992. David now lives completely within the presence of God and has been sharing his insights with all those who take the time to listen.

David has been teaching spiritual growth to a weekly class since 1987 and is demonstrating the depth of understanding present in a true spiritual master. This book is a result of that level of insight and understanding.

David can be contacted through the publisher, The Gnostic Wisdom Foundation.

Forward

More than half a million ancient texts have been recovered from the Middle East. Approximately 20% of those deal with religious issues, providing over 100,000 new religious texts from the ancient world. As these texts are being translated a radically new understanding of our religious past is emerging. Among those discoveries are *The Dead Sea Scrolls* and the *Nag Hammadi Scrolls* which are providing exciting new insights into the New Testament and the beginning years of the Christian faith. Other ancient texts are providing insights into the Old Testament and filling in many of the gaps in our own history and the development of the human race.

Because of the difficulty in reading the cuneiform text and recovering the writing on ancient scrolls, the task facing the scholars in translating the ancient knowledge is daunting, to say the least. While many of the scholars have religious training and backgrounds, this training sometimes makes it more difficult to perceive the exact meaning of these ancient texts because the tendency is to try to translate, or create an expression in our modern language that is not at odds with the religious beliefs of the scholar. As a result, some translations fail to make much sense and seem at odds with everything else. Most scholars agree that the ancient texts are enigmatic at best, and border on "unexplainable", based on our modern understanding of the world. As more and more of the ancient texts are translated and the information in them becomes more accepted, some, if not many, of the translations will need to be revised to reflect the newly emerging wealth of details and depth of understanding which is just now beginning to unfold.

We are indebted to the scholars for their dedication, knowledge and expertise in a difficult and demanding field. Their personal integrity and the integrity of their work is constantly being challenged by those who would have their own political or religious agenda supported and strengthened by ancient sources. The reality is many of our modern beliefs and religious foundations are not being borne out by the recovered texts. While a number of attempts have been, and are being, made to explain away the glaring differences between the ancient texts and our modern beliefs, we must, in the near future, come to terms with the veracity and integrity of the information being recovered.

The ancient world being revealed is surprisingly different from what we imagined it to be. A stunningly clear record of life in the ancient cities is emerging which portrays a civilization rivaling today's standards, encompassing an impressive educational system, legal tradition, and governmental organization not seen until the last two centuries of our modern history. And yet, the evidence, as disturbing as it is to the traditional view of history, documents in minute detail the workings of a thoroughly modern and refined civilization and social structure in existence for thousands of years before the Greek and Roman empires.

As disturbing as the discovery of a "modern" civilization in the time frame of 6,000 to 12,000 years ago may be, the impact of the ancient religious documents and texts upon the accepted doctrine of the modern church, mosque, or synagogue is no less than devastating. A new spiritual paradigm is emerging which encompasses both the ancient and modern texts in what is actually a very old spiritual perspective. Far from being ignorant pagans, our distant ancestors had a very impressive grasp and understanding of spiritual principles. This tradition has been passed down through the ages in the esoteric sayings and teachings of spiritual masters like Krishna, Buddha and Jesus.

The truth held in common among these diverse spiritual leaders is brought to life by a living spiritual master. Once we begin to grasp the hidden wisdom embedded in every religious system, we begin to understand they were all talking about the same thing. This universal spiritual truth forms the foundation of every religion and has been with us from the very beginning. Through the new spiritual paradigm the unification, not only of the self, but of mankind is possible. We stand now on the threshold of a new age of understanding and enlightenment. The secret knowledge of the past is not only revealed, but explained in modern terms and simple language so everyone can learn and experience the truth for themselves.

There is no mystery we cannot understand. We are dedicated to bringing the inner wisdom to all who will open their mind and heart and take their first real step into a larger world of awareness, perception, and consciousness. We hold to the principle that everyone is a divine child of God, created and constantly held in perfect equality, perfect love and perfect wholeness (holiness) in the mind of God. As such we are very pleased to bring you an example of this new spiritual paradigm in the form of an explanation of the sayings of Jesus in *The Gospel of Thomas.*

We hope you enjoy the work and insights of this author.

The Gnostic Wisdom Foundation

INTRODUCTION

The struggle for power and authority is basic to our human nature. Indeed, the history of the world is the story of that very quest: the conquering hero, the vanquished foe, and the resulting legends that feed the imagination of young and old alike. Especially in religion is the conflict glorified, the classic epic of good versus evil on a cosmic scale - eternal God and the rebellious Satan contending for the souls of mankind. How easily we get swept up in the rhetoric, pledging ourselves, believing, professing our faith, and drawing the battle lines here on Earth for the conflict that must surely come.

Only the bystander, the passer-by, dares to ask, "Are we the pawns, the prize, or the players in this contest?" Many are convinced that we are the prize of this cosmic conflict, always trying to do right and maintain our faith while constantly being seduced by Satan. Only those who truly believe and hold to their faith will be saved from eternal punishment. Others believe that we are pawns in this same conflict, the foot soldiers of God in an evil world, ever fighting for the souls of our fellow men. Still others believe that we are the players in the conflict, and while both good and evil things take place in the world, it is individual people that create the effect of good or evil by their own choices and actions.

Whatever our position, there is another issue that divides us even more. It slices through all other positions like Alexander the Great cleaving the Gordian knot with his sword. It cuts to the very heart of faith and religion. Framed as a question, it is this: Is the power of God something that is forever outside of us, or is it, as some claim, to be manifested within us? The question is not new; it has been with us from the beginning of time. Is power and authority ultimately to be vested within each individual, or must it always be placed in the hands of others? While this question is more readily answered in society based on levels of skills and resources, it becomes above all else a haunting and compelling spiritual question.

We have been well trained by modern religion to see God as an outside force - something to be worshipped, feared, and appealed to in times of trouble and distress. But it hasn't always been that way. Two millennia ago the landscape of religion was significantly different. Following the assassination of Julius Caesar in 44 BC,[1] two cities contended for domination of the known civilized world: Rome, the seat of political power represented by Octavian, and Alexandria in Egypt, the center of culture and religion, represented by Mark Antony. The military aspect of the conflict was brought to a close in 31 BC at the port of Actium on the western shore of Greece with Octavian's defeat of Mark Antony. Rome became the supreme center of political and military power.

While political power flowed from Rome, the cultural center of the known world was Alexandria in Egypt. Here the philosophers, religious, scientists, and artists of the world came to share their knowledge and wisdom with all who would listen and learn. The epicenter of this quest for spiritual and cultural enlightenment was the library, attached to the temple of Serapis, in the southern section of the city. Here, tens of thousands of documents recorded the accumulated knowledge and wisdom of mankind since the time of the Biblical flood. And it was here that the Gnostics reigned supreme. The ancient wisdom and tradition of the Egyptian mystery schools enjoyed prominent scholarly support, and the inner expression of Divinity was the standard of the day.

One hundred fifty to 200 years would pass before the rise of Christianity challenged the Gnostic system of religion. Early leaders of the Christian Church recognized that Rome was the center of political power and chose to align themselves with that power and authority. The marriage between the Christian Church and political power was formalized at the council of Nicea in 325 AD. Under the direction of the Emperor Constantine, bishops in the Christian Church ascended to the position of judges, with the military power of Rome at their disposal. Anything that differed from the approved Christian doctrine was deemed a heresy, and was to be destroyed.

Gnosticism (direct knowledge of God) was deemed a heresy by the Church and an aggressive program followed to rid the world of heretical documents. The final conflict between Rome and Alexandria came to a head in 391 AD[2], when Bishop Theophilus of Alexandria, under the Roman Emperor Theodosius I, led an angry mob of Christians across the city to the Temple of Serapis, destroying the statues, tapestries, artwork and icons in the temple and then focusing their rage on the library in the main wing of the temple, and in a day's time, destroyed the collected knowledge and wisdom of thousands of years. They burned all writings that did not agree with the doctrine of the Roman Christian Church. So it was that the center of religion was changed from Alexandria and its Gnostics to the Christians in Rome. God and divinity was relegated to outer, rather than inner expression.

The persecution of the Gnostics continued while foresighted individuals secreted copies of their sacred scriptures away, sealed in earthen jars, buried in eastern central Egypt, praying for the day when the ancient wisdom would once again be shared openly. Through this persecution and the deliberate destruction of sacred documents the Gospel of Thomas was "lost".

During the excavation of ruins in Oxyrhynchus, Egypt, in 1897 and 1903, over 5,000 fragments of ancient Greek texts were recovered from another ancient library. Among them were partial sections of what was believed to be the Gospel of Thomas. Due to a lack of other comparable documents, the discovery languished in the halls of academia through two world wars, remaining a curiosity and source of varied speculation.

In 1945, with the discovery of the buried earthen jars some 30 miles north of the Valley of the Kings near the town of Nag Hammadi, the world of the Gnostics sprang back to life as dozens of ancient Gnostic sacred scriptures were recovered. What became known as the "Nag Hammadi Scrolls" opened the door, releasing the "lost" ancient knowledge and wisdom again into the world. The two primary tasks were first to translate the ancient texts, and secondly to interpret the writings in modern terms so the people of our world could have access to the knowledge and wisdom that led to the presence of God - that which Jesus called "the Kingdom of Heaven" or "the Kingdom of God".

Once again the inner practice of divinity and spiritual growth is taking hold in the world, and once again the conflict between the inner expression of God and the belief in an outer being, separate from us, is being thrust upon the world of religion. In reading this explanation of the sayings of Jesus in the Gospel of Thomas, you will get an essentially Gnostic perception of Jesus, one contemporary with his life and experience in the first century. With this knowledge and understanding, you can determine which path, inner or outer, is right for you.

Unless otherwise indicated, we will be using the translation by Thomas O. Lambdin. Scholars generally agree the Gospel of Thomas is an esoteric text. In the traditional sense this means the understanding of the text is restricted to a very few. But the word "esoteric" also refers to inner, that which takes place within the mind and heart. This also makes esoteric teaching a system of inner transformation, which is how we will view the text. Following the sayings is a section explaining the exercises which will allow you to begin the process of transformation described in the sayings. Let us now take the gift of the scholars, the translation, and see what the inner path means to us today.

THE SAYINGS

These are the secret sayings which the living Jesus spoke and which Didymos Judas Thomas wrote down.

(1) And he said, "Whoever finds the interpretation of these sayings will not experience death."

Jesus said a number of unusual things. In Matthew 8:21, 22 (RSV) "Another of the disciples said to him, 'Lord, let me first go and bury my father.' But Jesus said to him, 'Follow me, and leave the dead to bury their own dead.'" Obviously, Jesus is referring to something other than corpses burying other corpses. So the concept of death he is using is dealing with something other than physical death.

In the ancient Gnostic and mystery school tradition, this kind of death had to do with the spirit within and with its consciousness. We are really dealing with two separate and distinct things: the spirit within us, and the ego or outer personality. One of the most important conversations in the New

Testament is in John, Chapter 3 (RSV), between two top leaders of the prime religious movements of the time, the Pharisees and the Gnostics. Here traditional Judaism meets and questions mystical Gnosticism. Nicodemus, a ruler of the Jews, comes to Jesus by night (the darkness represents ignorance), saying, "Rabbi, we know that you are a teacher come from God; for no one can do these signs that you do, unless God is with him." Jesus answered him, "Truly, truly, I say to you, unless one is born anew (or from above), he cannot see the Kingdom of God." Nicodemus said to him, "How can a man be born when he is old? Can he enter a second time into his mother's womb and be born?" Jesus answered, "Truly, truly, I say to you, unless one is born of water and the Spirit, he cannot enter the Kingdom of God. That which is born of the flesh is flesh, and that which is born of the Spirit is spirit."

Here Jesus clearly defines two separate and distinct things. That which is born of the flesh is flesh. Our ego, or outer personality, is born of the flesh. It is called the false self or corrupted nature in the Gnostic system. That which is born of the Spirit is spirit. This is the true self, incorruptible and eternal. Notice that the first use of Spirit is capitalized, while the second spirit is not. The capitalized Spirit refers to God, the Creator, while the other spirit refers to that which is in each of us, our personal spirit. We are created in the image of God. On a practical level, this means that God created us out of God substance (spirit); just as a woman brings forth a child from her own substance, so too has God brought forth each of us from His own substance. The source of all life is Spirit (God), and everything that lives has some of that substance of God in it. The spirit within each of us is an individualized expression of the Spirit that is God.

In the Gnostic system a person was considered spiritually dead until their spirit was awakened. The awakening and empowerment of the spirit was referred to as resurrection, or being raised up from the dead, and applied only to the spirit within, not the physical body. This is why Jesus says "leave the dead to bury their own dead." As long as the consciousness is attached to the ego, or outer personality, it is temporary; it has no real life of its own. It is only when consciousness is attached to the spirit that it gains permanent status, for only the spirit remains alive after physical death. When people die do we not say "they are gone"? Clearly the body is still there. We can see it, we can touch it. So what is gone? The spirit, the God substance, our personal source of life is gone, not the body.

So, "whoever finds the interpretation of these sayings will not experience death" describes the result of the process of moving the attachment of consciousness from the ego over to the spirit. In this process the spirit becomes awakened from its deep sleep, grows, matures, and takes its place as a mature spiritual being operating fully and completely in the presence of God (which Jesus often calls "the Kingdom").

(2) Jesus said, "Let him who seeks continue seeking until he finds. When he finds, he will become troubled. When he becomes troubled, he will be astonished, and he will rule over the all."

Here the Greek version differs somewhat from the Coptic, so we will consider it as well.

> **[Jesus said,] "Let the one seek[ing] not stop [seeking until] he finds. And when he find[s he will marvel, and mar]veling he will reign, an[d reigning] he will [rest.]"**

This is the essence of the Gnostic experience. It is a quest, a journey without distance. The point is that it is not about believing; it is about an ongoing process, a search for truth, a search for answers about our true nature, our true origins, and our Creator. The ultimate goal of the search is to find God. As is the case in all true spiritual journeys, the answers we find are not what we expect, or desire. The truth is rarely wanted, or really desired, and yet, as Jesus has told us, the truth will set us free.

Most of us do not really want to know the truth, what we want is to have what we already believe to become the truth, or to be confirmed as truth. Either way, as we seek, and continue to seek, we will discover things about God, ourselves, and the world in which we live that are contrary to what we have been taught and have come to believe. A true spiritual path will take us to the depths of our inner being, our belief system, our assumptions and conclusions, and will shine the light of truth on every facet of who we think we are. The answers we receive as a result of our continuing search will shake the foundations of every belief we have. This is at first very disturbing, but through our willingness to change, a greater truth and a resulting blessing will become manifest in our lives.

The Gnostic process is one of creating direct experiences with the presence of God. Those experiences bring an in-depth understanding, step by step, about the nature of God, our creation, our true nature, and the exotic process we have begun. What we learn from this direct experience is often counter to the traditional teachings of religion. For example, religion teaches that God is jealous and vengeful and that God will judge us (usually harshly) for any and all transgressions during our lives. And yet one of the experiences we have along the way in our spiritual growth is of the unconditional love that comes directly from God. In this experience we discover that this is not an intellectual revelation, as we might expect, but rather a profound, deeply moving, emotional experience. I have yet to meet someone who has experienced this love that comes directly from God that has not been moved completely to tears. It is one of the most intense experiences in life. What we realize after this experience is that there was no judgment from God at all. Of all the condemnations we have received from others, and of particular importance, from our own ego, none of them materialize in this intense experience of God's love for us.

Have we not done things that are improper, demanding judgment in some form, if not from the world then certainly from God? How can it be that we receive unconditional love in place of punishment? This contradicts what we have been taught about God. This experience of unconditional love, especially an experience this intense, shakes our belief in judgment and punishment from God to the very core of our being. Once this realization sinks into our consciousness, our very concept of God is challenged. We find ourselves asking the same question that Nicodemus asked, "How can this be?"

Were this experience of unconditional love an isolated incidence, we could dismiss it as an aberration. But it is not the only experience we encounter; other experiences bring us a deep abiding sense of peace, an inner joy, serenity, and a connectedness with God on a very personal level. These other experiences are consistent with the unconditional love that we receive from God. Totally absent is any form of judgment, criticism or punishment. The disturbing shock to our belief in a God of judgment gradually gives way to the reality of a loving, gentle God of Spirit, hope, and eternal life. In time we find ourselves becoming an integral part of the oneness that is God and creation together, a vibrant individual in an interactive universe - one conscious element in an ocean of consciousness, a mature spiritual being functioning fully and completely in the presence of God. We find ourselves not only living in the presence of God, but functioning as an active, directive force with the complete resources of God at our disposal.

This direct experience of the presence of God is the central core of the Gnostic experience and the transformational power of the teachings of Jesus. It is not a factor of belief or faith. It is the result of an intimate, repeated inner experience that leaves no room for doubt. We do not have to believe, for we have experienced the presence of God for ourselves. We do not have to have faith, for we are living the experience day after day. It is not what we think; it is what we know as a result of our direct experience with God.

The Coptic version adds; "an[d reigning] he will [rest.]" Our own ego perceives "reigning" and "ruling" as the ultimate power and authority over others. Yet as we become one with God and creation, we find that it is not others that need to be ruled over, it is our own lower nature, the domain of the ego itself. In oneness we see that others are not in need of being ruled as much as they are in need of being educated and enlightened. We as a species need help, not judgment or punishment. The "rest" spoken of here is the deep abiding peace of God, the serenity that comes with the presence of God in our lives. It is not a withdrawal from life and society, but an understanding of the basic human need for God that fills us with compassion, gentleness, kindness and respect for each and every creature in creation. We become more connected, more integrated into the fabric of humanity, and more determined to teach and help. Our desire and commitment rests in the certainty of God's presence and unconditional love. There is no greater peace. There is no greater power.

(3) Jesus said, "If those who lead you say to you, 'See, the kingdom is in the sky,' then the birds of the sky will precede you. If they say to you, 'It is in the sea,' then the fish will precede you. Rather, the kingdom is inside of you, and it is outside of you. When you come to know yourselves, then you will become known, and you will realize that it is you who are the sons of the living father. But if you will not know yourselves, you dwell in poverty and it is you who are that poverty."

Many of us have been taught that God's Kingdom is a place we go when we die. A quick survey of conditions here on earth certainly tends to support the notion that heaven must be somewhere else. This can't be it. So if it isn't here, where is it? Heaven is traditionally placed high in the sky, but Jesus is telling us that is not correct. First of all Jesus is telling us it is not a place. So if the Kingdom is not a place, then what is it?

As we will see as we continue through the Gospel of Thomas, the Kingdom is actually a state of consciousness. As such, it will not come of its own accord. It is not a collective experience that will happen to everyone at some point in time; it is an individual experience that must be entered into. Jesus told us in the traditional gospels that the Kingdom of Heaven was at hand, meaning close by, within reach, something that can be grasped. If the Kingdom really was a place or a time, it should have been found or have arrived long ago. But if the Kingdom is a state of consciousness, we can begin to understand how it can be so close, and yet so far away. A state of consciousness can be close by, within reach, and can be grasped, but only through the effort of the individual. A person can be placed in a room where everyone else in the room shares a specific consciousness, and yet that individual may not have a clue.

Jesus is telling us that the specific effort required to enter into this Kingdom is in learning to know ourselves. If we are unwilling, or unable, to know ourselves, then we can progress no further; the Kingdom will be denied to us. There is also another element being expressed, that of being found, which we will explore more in the parable of the lost sheep (saying #107). It is our search, and more importantly, our dedication to the search, that brings us to the attention of God. We do not enter into the Kingdom solely on our own efforts, for it is a co-operative process with God. We embark on a specific path of learning, experiencing, and realizing that gradually transforms us, raising our level of knowledge, understanding, and wisdom, until our mind, heart and spirit have been raised up, entering into higher and higher levels of consciousness, until we find ourselves in a state of oneness with God and all of creation. This is the Kingdom, this state of oneness, this condition of 100% full conscious contact with God, a condition we now call the 'Christ Consciousness'. In this consciousness we take our rightful place as mature children of God – "sons" of the living father, spirit created out of Spirit, true spiritual beings, forever living in the presence of God.

Consciousness is not something that is simply in our head or mind. It is more than just "inside" us. In some spiritual systems, once a person has progressed to a certain level, there is no longer an oral or written form of instruction. The student simply spends a number of hours each day sitting and meditating in the presence of the master. There develops a shared consciousness and in that process the student enters into, and experiences, higher states of consciousness accessible only by the spiritual master. The resulting shared experience educates the student in a way unattainable by any other means.

The other interesting facet is that when people have the experience of this higher state of consciousness they share so many common elements with others that have experienced the same state, that it is usually expressed as the one or highest truth. It doesn't seem to matter which spiritual system is used; the end result is remarkably similar. The experience provides us with a deep and unshakable knowledge that life goes on. After this experience, it is common for people to lose their fear of death. Calmness takes the place of fear. It is not a matter of believing; it is a knowing, a certainty, a fact already proven. It becomes the cornerstone of their life, transforming the mundane into the sublime.

But if we will not put forth the effort and learn these inner things about ourselves and for ourselves, we remain in ignorance. We become prey to fantasies, lies and superstition. Our only hope is to believe and blindly follow someone else, trusting that they know something we do not, having faith that they will not betray us. In the end we are always disappointed, for it really is a case of the blind leading the blind. Only through our own personal experiences in the presence of God can we truly come to know the truth, and it is only through knowing the truth that we can set ourselves free.

(4) Jesus said, "The man old in days will not hesitate to ask a small child seven days old about the place in life, and he will live. For many who are first will become last, and they will become one and the same."

We must remember that this is an inner (esoteric) teaching and process. The inner experience of the presence of God is not very common, so the primary way we have of explaining these inner things is to use outer examples which people have in common. Anyone that has been around a seven day old infant knows this saying cannot be taken literally. So what is Jesus saying?

If we look at the experience of being "born again" as a true inner awakening of the spirit, we find a number of things taking place. Our perception of the world changes radically. Everything seems "new", as if we were seeing it clearly for the first time. Colors are much more intense, the senses of touch and hearing are enhanced, as are taste and smell. It is like waking from a deep sleep, and seeing the world for the first time. As you experience this spiritual awakening you really get "a feel" for why it is called "being born again". It is an exciting, exhilarating experience. You feel truly alive for the first time in your life.

There is a clarity of perception that comes with being born again. The purpose and nature of life are clear; everything has fallen into place. The man old in days is the ego, and the small child, seven days old is the newly awakened spirit within. The revelations of this experience come rapidly. Some comments this author has received from people going through this awakening experience are: "This is the only game in town. I don't see why everybody isn't doing it" and "This is wonderful. We have to tell everyone about this."

This is the time that the ego gets caught up in the excitement and wants to be part of what is happening. The ego wants to know its place in the process. This is also a challenging time for the ego, for it soon discovers that it will not be the star, receiving the glory and power of spiritual empowerment. This is where John, chapter 3 continues (3:28 RSV), "You yourselves bear me witness, that I said, I am not the Christ, but I have been sent before him. He who has the bride is the bridegroom; the friend of the bridegroom, who stands and hears him, rejoices greatly at the bridegroom's voice; therefore this joy of mine is now full. He must increase, but I must decrease."

Here is the final realization of the ego: it is not the spirit. It is what has come before, and it must decrease so that the spirit may grow, mature, and become empowered. The ego now hears the voice of the spirit within and begins to see its role clearly. The ego now recognizes its purpose and the ultimate sacrifice it must perform. John 3:31, "He who comes from above is above all; he who is of the earth belongs to the earth, and of the earth he speaks; he who comes from heaven is above all." The ego now recognizes that it is temporal, part of the physical body (of the earth), and really knows only about physical life. But the spirit is of God (comes from above) and is eternal. John 3:35, "The Father loves the Son, and has given all things into his hand." It is the spirit within us that is the Son, and receives the things of God.

The ego comes first and must become last. In the end the ego surrenders completely and is merged into the spirit. The two become one and the same. The separation of the spirit and the ego is experienced as the separation of us from God. It is why God initially appears as an entity outside of us. It is only when the separation within is healed, and the ego and spirit become one that we also become one with God. Separation is separation from everything: each other, God, nature, eternal life. Oneness is the result of inner healing, and it is oneness with everything. We cannot be "one with God" and still perceive other people as being separate. Nor can we be "one with God" and still perceive anything in nature as being separate. Oneness is oneness, it is total and complete or it is not real oneness.

(5) Jesus said, "Recognize what is in your sight, and that which is hidden from you will become plain to you. For there is nothing hidden which will not become manifest."

The inner teaching begins with the recognition that there is more to us than we have perceived. A spiritual path is often referred to as a journey without distance because it is the journey of self discovery. As we grow from childhood into adulthood, the ego grows along with us. We come to assume that the ego *is* us, and we are it. The ego presents itself as whole, complete; there is nothing else. And yet a simple exercise opens an inner door and reveals the existence of something more than the ego and its thoughts.

Pause for a few moments and close your eyes. Observe the thoughts that pass through your mind. Many times we will begin to recognize how thoughts are connected, one to the next. Some element of one thought acts as a string to the next thought, and on and on it goes. You may even have a thought about how all this works, even as the thoughts being observed continue on uninterrupted. The question is this. If the thoughts being observed are the activities of my mind, what is doing the observing? Is the mind observing itself or is something else going on? The classic question in this example is, "Who is the observer?"

While some people see this as utter nonsense, others see an opening into another level of perception, a new area of exploration and experience. Those which follow this new lead sometimes feel like they have followed Alice through the rabbit hole into a strange new world where nothing really is as it seems to be. Everything we have come to know and trust is now called into question. In this journey of self discovery we come to see ourselves as fractured pieces, held together by invisible buffers. Programming and imprinting from parents, relatives, friends, teachers, authority figures and mentors are all there, each in its own little world, like pieces of a jig-saw puzzle. The task of self discovery is to explore each of these pieces, determine the value each presents, and discard the valueless. In this way the individual pieces can be joined and the inner separation can be healed. This leads to wholeness, holiness, and oneness.

With a little education about the mind and consciousness, we gradually begin to recognize what has been in front of us all along. We see the fractured nature of the ego's world and how it pulls and pushes us through the everyday experiences of life. We discover why we are stressed by a situation where someone else doesn't seem to even notice that it exists. We come to see that we really are individuals, that no two of us are exactly alike. Our thoughts, feelings and perceptions are all different, even given the same external circumstances.

As we come to recognize the various parts of our personality, we gradually uncover the inner nature of the spirit within. This is the part that was hidden, and through the process of self discovery, becomes revealed. As we learn more about the spirit within, we see in it the answer to life's question, "Is this all there is?" The body and the ego that results are limited and temporal. The spirit within is unlimited and eternal. But until we actually begin the process of self discovery, the inner world remains hidden. The ego tells us, "Go out into the world and find the answer – seek and you will find!" But the answer is not "out there", it is within.

(6) His disciples questioned Him and said to Him, "Do you want us to fast? How shall we pray? Shall we give alms? What diet shall we observe?" Jesus said, "Do not tell lies, and do not do what you hate, for all things are plain in the sight of Heaven. For nothing hidden will not become manifest, and nothing covered will remain without being uncovered."

The questions on fasting, prayer, alms and diet are partially answered in saying #14 below, so we will split the explanation, addressing different facets in each case.

Fasting, the form and time of prayer, the giving of alms, and specific dietary restrictions are all part of the religious system in which the disciples were raised and well trained. Jesus is constantly being questioned about these things. If we look at a little history, we can begin to grasp why the questions were being asked, and what impact the answers might have had.

Alexander the Great conquered the Middle East area around 327 BC and left a number of local "kings" in charge to keep the peace and to collect taxes (tribute). These were the Seleucid kings. By the late third century BC, the Maccabee rebellion was taking place. The Maccabees were a fundamentalist Judeo faction dedicated to the use of military force to restore freedom in Judea. A splinter group, disenchanted with the use of military force, left the Maccabees around 200 BC, going off into the desert to seek God. This group floundered for about 20 years until the arrival of an individual from the mystery school system. This individual became known as "the teacher of righteousness" and the group is now known as the Essenes.

The Essene community was located on the northwest shore of the Dead Sea, and the Essenes are the authors of the 'Dead Sea Scrolls'. The Dead Sea Scrolls are an eclectic mixture of fundamentalist Judaism and concepts from the mystery school tradition. It is this mixture, blended with some Gnostic features that form the early foundation for Christianity.

Also emanating from Egypt were the Gnostics, a direct outreach program of the mystery school system. So there were three main religious factions working the area of Judea at the time of Jesus (the Pharisees and Sadducees being branches of Judaism). The questions being asked were designed to clarify which of these religious factions were being represented. The differences may not be as clear as we might think, for the three systems are inter-related. The Torah, for example, was used by all three systems. Strict rules for fasting, prayer, alms and diet are part of the Judaic religion, being slightly relaxed with the Essenes, and significantly different with the Gnostics. The answers given by Jesus in saying #14 clearly identify his teachings with the Gnostics.

Jesus said, "Do not tell lies, and do not do what you hate, for all things are plain in the sight of heaven." The ego seeks all the advantages it can find in the world. It learns early on in childhood that there are some advantages to lying and doing things that you really don't want to do. Women especially are encouraged by the images and expectations of modern society to do things that they would rather not do, and present themselves in ways they are really not comfortable with for the sake of appearances and relationships. These things have a costly internal toll on our self image and self respect. The cost is already too high if we consider only the ego or personality, but as we factor in the emerging spirit, the inner conflict can become severe.

The process of spiritual growth not only requires, but also demands honesty and truthfulness within. Indeed, no true spiritual growth can take place when it is based on any kind of falsehood. A true spiritual path is, above all else, a quest for truth. In continuing lies for the advancement in financial or social and political conditions, we are undermining and destroying the spirit within. We are sacrificing the eternal for the temporal.

We think that how we feel on the inside, or what we privately believe about ourselves or others, does not, and will not, show on the outside. Watch the eyes and facial features of people around you. With a little practice you will see what is going on in their lives. It has been said that people live lives of quiet desperation. You will discover that this is true; you can see it in their faces. Once you recognize the quiet desperation in others, the day will come when you see it in your own face in the mirror. This is our legacy in the world of the ego; none will escape. All of the hidden feelings, beliefs, guilt and pain are painted on our faces for all to see.

The only workable answer is to abandon the ego and its ways in favor of the spirit. Methodically replacing each falsehood with truth, each condemnation with forgiveness, each injury with kindness, each hate with compassion, and each fear with love transforms the inner experience from desperation to joy. This too becomes painted on our face. Peace, love and joy are the hallmarks of real spiritual growth and there is no way to hide them from others.

Spiritual truths will also begin coming to us. There is no spiritual mystery which we cannot know. The closer we come to God, the more of the spiritual mysteries and principles we will encounter. All the Father has is given to the Son. There is no spiritual truth which will not be revealed to us. Piece by piece, step by step, the whole will be revealed. Once we reach this 100% full conscious contact with God we will have access to every spiritual truth and principle. Nothing will remain hidden.

(7) Jesus said, "Blessed is the lion which becomes man when consumed by man, and cursed is the man whom the lion consumes, and the lion becomes man."

Life is a process of transformation. Nothing really remains the same. The seed sprouts, becomes a seedling, a small tree, a large tree, and in time succumbs to disease, fire or cutting and becomes something else. People change. Time changes us, and if nothing else, life itself will change us; but into what? Are we grist for the mill, unable to alter the end result, or are we active selectors of the outcome? In terms of religion, are we poor helpless sinners, dependant on God's grace for salvation, or are we free and independent spiritual children here to work out our own growth and ultimate salvation?

In spiritual terms, generally we have two options: to be spirit guided or ego guided. In being guided by the ego, as we all are as we grow up in the world, the body and the ego are dominant factors in our life. This is the essentially carnal life, the dark side of which is unrestrained lust, greed and violence. The lighter side appears more civilized on the surface, with the finer trappings of wealth, high society and social graces. Yet under the surface the same basic driving forces of the ego are at work, the hidden animal nature that establishes territory and pecking orders, domination, submission and control. This is the lion, the beast, the hidden controller of our lives.

As we examine the actual performance of our society we can come to the conclusion that we are still a barbaric people with a thin veneer of civility. The crimes we commit against each other, the injustices we allow, the adoration of the predators among us, and the disgust for the poor and downtrodden are all primary indicators of the ego at work. Competition, the survival of the fittest - these are the rally cries of the ego. War is the ultimate competition, where we really do bury the opposition.

We need to ask. Is there another way, a better way? And if there is, what needs to be done to accomplish it? This is what the spiritual path ostensibly offers: the higher path of cooperation in place of competition, respect in place of control, and compassion in place of condemnation and conflict. So how do we change the world into that kinder, gentler place? The answer is that we must begin by changing ourself first. We can change nothing else until we have become transformed, and then, by teaching the same process of transformation to others, we can extend our experience out into the world, changing it at the most fundamental level, one person at a time.

Transformation will happen to us, either through the ego by default, or through the spirit by choice and dedication. Knowing that choices need to be made, and knowing what the outcomes of those choices are, become the essential factors for making informed decisions. Many times we cannot know these factors, but, here, we are more fortunate; these choices have been made before by many people, and the results are available for us to examine.

If we allow the ego and its animal nature to rule our lives we will be consumed by its desires and obsessions, ultimately left empty because the fires of the ego consume the soul as fire consumes its fuel. Being consumed by this lion is the curse of mankind.

Yet there are those, like Jesus, who have taken a different path, and in doing so, have experienced something extraordinary, and they have tried to share that experience with others. They have told us that they have found eternal life, and have come into the full and complete presence of God. We marvel at the things they tell us and wonder if it could really be true. We have been deceived before and are now wary of such claims. Do we believe them or not?

In the outer form of religion the person having this extraordinary experience is transformed into a savior, and believing in this savior brings salvation. But in the inner form we become transformed, and that transformation becomes our salvation. Belief is not required, just hard work and dedication. The real question becomes, do we believe the teacher and understand the teaching enough to actually begin the process of transformation? Do we dare follow Jesus and become like him, or do we take the path of little or no risk and just believe?

The problem in simply believing is that the ego is still in control of our lives. We are still consumed by the lion. Only by going through the transformational process is the animal nature within removed from empowerment, taken apart, and consumed. This transformation that Jesus teaches dissolves the ego and empowers the spirit, bringing us into the same extraordinary experience He is having. Do we dare live in the presence of God? Do we really want to be blessed, or are we more comfortable being cursed? These are difficult questions, but it is necessary to answer them before the transformational process can begin.

(8) And He said, "The man is like a wise fisherman who cast his net into the sea and drew it up from the sea full of small fish. Among them the wise fisherman found a fine large fish. He threw all the small fish back into the sea and chose the large fish without difficulty. Whoever has ears to hear, let him hear."

Fish represent ideas or concepts. The world, like the sea full of fish, is full of ideas, the vast majority of which are small. The trick is to find the fine large fish or idea, and discard the small ones. With fish, this is easy; we can see the difference. But with ideas it is difficult to "see" the difference. The problem is, the ego has perception only in the world; it is of the world, and in the world it must remain. Therefore, spiritual ideals appear as small ideas of questionable value. Money, power, position, appear as big ideas to the ego, and as we are beginning to understand, these ideas will ultimately consume us.

But this is a *wise* fisherman, and it is his wisdom which allows him to perceive the really great idea among the rest. With wisdom we can select the great idea without difficulty. So how do we get wisdom? There was a comment about this making its way around the internet. It said, "Wisdom comes on the arm of age, but sometimes age comes alone." In many cultures the elders are considered wise. So does this mean that we have to wait until we are old? As we can discern for ourselves, age alone is not a grantor of wisdom. So what is?

Wisdom is a function of understanding tempered by experience. In life we have come to see the value of education, and the knowledge that can be gained through learning. Once we "complete" our education we begin our career and put our knowledge to work for us. It is through the application of knowledge that we gain understanding, and the re-evaluation of our understandings based on new insights brings experience. Wisdom, like spiritual growth, is the result of a process. But processes are like ideas; the world is full of them. Again, how do we know?

The subject of wisdom and how to acquire it is a repetitive theme in the Gospel of Thomas. We will explore it in more depth in sayings 21, 28, 34, 43, and 45.

(9) Jesus said, "Now the sower went out, took a handful (of seeds), and scattered them. Some fell on the road; the birds came and gathered them up. Others fell on rock, did not take root in the soil, and did not produce ears. And others fell on thorns; they choked the seed(s) and worms ate them. And others fell on good soil and produced good fruit; it bore sixty per measure and a hundred and twenty per measure."

Seeds also represent ideas. In spiritual work a person must have an open mind and be willing to learn and examine new ideas. Spiritual growth is a step-by-step process where information, concepts and understanding are built one piece at a time. We test to see if a person is ready for this process by providing a small piece of information, or a small concept and observing how the person handles it. We call this process "planting a seed".

People process this new information or concept in several ways, depending on "where they are coming from" in their attitude, belief system or general consciousness. Most people are committed to the mainstream consensus of thought. This is represented by the "road", which is well traveled. In some versions of the sower parable this is a path instead of a road. The connotation is essentially the same; it is where most of the people travel: mainstream thought. If the seeds, the information or concept presented, are not "mainstream" then there is no place for the idea to take root, to be accepted. The defense mechanisms of the mind are represented by the birds. Anything not conforming to the mainstream point of view is attacked and removed from the mind and consciousness. The established order must be maintained.

Some of the seeds fell on rocks. Rocks are firmly held beliefs. This is common in strictly religious people. The new idea is in conflict with the established doctrine, and because of the firmly held beliefs, there is no room for the new idea or information to take root - to be accepted.

Some seeds fell on thorns. Thorns are competing ideas. The ego, being of the earth cannot tell the difference between a false idea and a true one. They all appear to have at least equal value, or in many cases, the false ideas are structured to be more attractive to the ego than is the truth. The true path requires work and dedication and persistent effort to produce results. False paths generally require only acceptance of the ideas, or professed belief in the doctrine presented.

Each of us has had at least some experience with this. Who among us, when faced with something which is perceived as a lot of work, has not asked "isn't there an easier way; a shortcut?" Each false path is presented as a "shortcut", a quick easy way of accomplishing the same thing. In our experience of the way things work in the world, "if it sounds too good to be true", then there is cause to be more than a little suspicious. Many people spend their lives looking for the "shortcut" in everything. In the end they have nothing. The wise among us realize that real success comes from hard work and dedication to our goals, not shortcuts. The "easy" way is to do it right the first time, so you don't have to do it over and over again. The competing ideas, the shortcuts, consume all of the time and energy, leaving nothing for working the true path. The seeds are thus choked out, and the "worms", disparaging thoughts and comments, consume the new idea.

Some people have an open mind and are willing to consider new information and new concepts. Here the seeds fall on good soil and take root. The ideas are accepted and become the foundation of a new action plan to produce results. In the path of spiritual growth this is the beginning of the work of self discovery and the transformation that will follow. The mature spiritual individual and the effect that individual has on others around them is represented by the good fruit. The transformed individual becomes love-based, treating everyone with respect, gentleness, and kindness. The loving nature of this individual touches the minds and hearts of others, and in their quest to be of service to others, the overall quality of life in the community is improved. This individual enters into the extraordinary experience of living in the presence of God and everything around them responds in kind.

(10) Jesus said, "I have cast fire upon the world, and see, I am guarding it until it blazes."

In the 1960's, Zen was becoming popular. Many people didn't understand how an eastern religion could become so attractive to people and how it could generate so much interest. The answer resided not in the religion, but in the monks and priests who came here and shared their experiences. Mainstream Christianity is an outer form of religion based on believing. The focus is on the dogma of the church and the conformity to doctrine as presented by the clergy. Zen is more of an inner form of religion, and those who have progressed well into the transformational process were the representatives of Zen with whom the people of America came into contact.

For the first time in many people's lives, they came into direct contact with someone transformed through this extraordinary inner experience. The peace, love and joy of the presence of God within was so obvious that people very quickly recognized Zen as a living religion - not just something to be believed, but a living, breathing experience of the presence of God. Many eastern religions talk about the divine spark or flame within. This appears in both inner and outer forms of religion. The difference with the inner form is that one not only believes in this inner flame, but actually experiences it and is involved in the process of making it grow.

We have become familiar, at least to a degree, with the "fire in the belly" from some motivational speakers. It is a phrase descriptive of a burning desire to accomplish a specific goal. This burning desire is a function of the ego and is instrumental in creating success in business, politics and other endeavors in the world. There is a spiritual counterpart: the awakened spirit within. It, too, burns within, but its attention is not on accomplishing the things of the world; rather it is focused on becoming one with God and everything else. As the transformational experience progresses, the spirit within becomes stronger and the light of the divine flame expands. This inner light of living in the presence of God is exceptionally moving to people when they come into contact with it and it was the attraction of Zen.

Christianity also has an inner teaching and tradition, and the effect is identical. The teachings of Jesus, when understood from the inner perspective, lead us on that inner journey of self-discovery and spiritual growth. Awakening the spirit, feeding it from the love-based emotions that we can all generate, and raising it up to a position of power and authority in our lives expands the inner light, embeds us in the Kingdom of Heaven, and places us firmly in the presence of God. The light of spirit and the love which comes from God, flowing through us out into the world, is the fire Jesus has cast upon the world.

This fire of spiritual light and love does not come overnight. It is the result of the inner journey of self-discovery and spiritual growth. It is the outer sign of the transformational process within, a process that takes time, effort and dedication. This is why the fire must by guarded until it blazes. It does not happen on its own; it is the result of a great deal of inner work, guided by a true spiritual teacher who can nurture and guide the mind and heart as they come together with the spirit to form an inner trinity. Once a person has progressed to a higher level of understanding in the transformational process, the world can no longer trample the inner flame. Then, it is safe to let the light shine. That person becomes a guiding light for others, spreading the fire which Jesus cast upon the world so many years ago.

(11) Jesus said, "This heaven will pass away, and the one above it will pass away. The dead are not alive, and the living will not die. In the days when you consumed what is dead, you made it what is alive. When you come to dwell in the light, what will you do? On the day when you were one you became two. But when you become two, what will you do?"

Something special happens during the process of physical conception. Just before the sperm fertilizes the egg the light of spirit appears. Without the light and presence of spirit, fertilization does not take place. Spirit is the source of life and without it nothing lives. In this example it is easier for us to see that we begin as one thing - spirit, and through the process of placing the living light of spirit around the sperm and egg, enabling fertilization, we become two things – a spirit and a physical body. The two are inexorably linked until the moment of death.

During pregnancy the fetus develops and is imprinted by sounds, movement and emotions. Here in the womb, the developing person begins its relationship with the world. As birth takes place, the attention is focused on making the body move as desired and exploring the outer world. In the child's quest to discover and experience the outer world, the ego develops and the inner spirit gradually goes to sleep. During this time we identify ourselves with the ego, our consciousness becomes attached to the ego and from that point, we perceive ourselves as a single identity, the ego and its physical reality, the body, being as one.

Through our introduction to the inner path of spiritual growth, we discover that we are really two things, not just the one which we have previously perceived. When we discover this dual reality the question really does become "What do I do now?" It is uncomfortable for us to remain in duality like this. We have an inner need to function as a complete unit. Duality implies part of us is not under control. It is disturbing. Something needs to be done, but what? What will we do? The ego tries to ignore the situation, but it is always there in the back of our mind. What will we do?

Only the inner spiritual path holds a lasting resolution to the question, "what will you do?" For only through inner transformation can the two become one. Through this inner transformation we come to live in the presence of God, in the light of Spirit, but once we have come to dwell in the light, then what do we do? Everything has changed. The goals and desires we had in the world are no more. We are now connected with God and all of God's creation, lovingly attached to other people as we see the spirit within each of them. Most shocking about this new connectedness is how other people can exist in this vast ocean of God, like fish in the sea, and be unaware of its existence.

Again the question, "What will you do?" needs to be answered. In the letter of James (RSV) 2:14-17 James says, "What does it profit, my brethren, if a man says he has faith but has no works? Can his faith save him? If a brother or sister is ill-clad and in lack of daily food, and one of you says to them, 'Go in peace, be warmed and filled,' without giving them the things needed for the body, what does it profit? So faith by itself, if it has no works, is dead."

The ego sees others as separate, and competing with us for limited goods and services. It is justified in paying lip service to others but not in giving of ourselves to improve the conditions of someone else without receiving something in return. The spirit sees others as brothers and sisters, as part of the connected whole, where when one is diminished the whole is diminished. "What will you do" calls us into action, not just because it is the right thing to do, but because the emerging state of love and compassion within us compels us to improve the quality of life of others in whatever way we can.

Jesus, in Matthew 25:35-40 (RSV) is trying to teach the disciples about how our changed state changes our level of action and responsibility. He states, "for I was hungry and you gave me food, I was thirsty and you gave me drink, I was a stranger and you welcomed me, I was naked and you clothed me, I was sick and you visited me, I was in prison and you came to me." Then the righteous will answer him, "Lord, when did we see thee hungry and feed thee, or thirsty and give thee drink? And when did we see thee a stranger and welcome thee, or naked and clothe thee? And when did we see thee sick or in prison and visit thee?" And the king will answer them, "Truly, I say to you, as you did it to one of the least of these my brethren, you did it to me."

The ego, in its separation, will not extend itself to truly care for others. Only the spirit, functioning from oneness is compelled to act, to make a difference in the lives of others. For many people, what they really want out of their lives is to make a difference. The ego sees that difference as something great and profound, something that changes the course of human history. Because the perceived task is monumental, very few even try. But the spirit sees the small ways to make a difference in the world, by making a small difference in an individual life. If each of us would do only one thing to improve the quality of life for one person, even if only for a short period of time, the world as we know it would be transformed overnight.

Once we understand that it is the small, personal things that really make a difference in life, we have opened the door to the means of changing the world. It is the deeper understanding of our selves (self-discovery) that opens us up to understanding others. While we can share what we have with others, we soon learn that the most important thing we have is our connection with God. And this is something that can be taught, in essence given away without diminishing anyone. In fact, the more we share our experiences and insights, the greater the blessings become.

We feel compelled to talk to other people about our experience and convince them to go through this process and enter the oneness for themselves. After alienating a number of friends and relatives through our enthusiasm, we realize that something different must be done to bring this experience to others. With a deeper understanding of human nature we learn to adopt the method of planting "seeds" and evaluating which people are open-minded enough to receive more information and ideas. As we go through this learning curve we gradually make the transition from student to teacher, sharing the information, concepts and experiences with others on a regular basis.

Through our education and transformation, our past perceptions of heaven give way and are replaced by personal experiences and individual spiritual insights. Over time these initial experiences and insights are again replaced with deeper understanding and wisdom. We clearly see it is spirit that is the source of all life. The body is not alive separate from the spirit, and the living spirit will not die.

(12) The disciples said to Jesus, "We know that you will depart from us. Who is to be our leader? Jesus said to them, "Wherever you are, you are to go to James the righteous, for whose sake heaven and earth came into being."

James the Righteous, or James the Just, is presented as the brother of Jesus. It is this James who becomes the head of the Essene community, and after a popular rebellion in Jerusalem, ascends to the position of high priest in the temple in Jerusalem. It also appears this James is responsible for at least the content of the letter of James in the New Testament. The comments about the necessity for "works" as opposed to "faith" are revealing of the inner path as opposed to the outer form of believing.

James, as high priest, takes on the form of the elevated spiritual man, in Gnostic terms "the Son of man". The upper case "Son" denotes the awakened, elevated spiritual being within, while the lower case version denotes the sleeping, dormant spirit within the ego-based individual. In essence, all of creation has been constructed for the purpose of providing an environment where the individual spirit can grow and mature. Through the interaction with the world the living spirit within eventually determines what it is and what it is not, refining its perception of reality, separating truth from falsehood, and gaining strength, understanding and wisdom. James, the high priest, represents, in a single person, the spiritual essence of all of us. The high priest, representing all of us, prayed for forgiveness on the Day of Atonement in the "holy of holies", the inner chamber of the temple in Jerusalem. For all of us, represented by James, heaven and earth have come into existence.

This outer practice is symbolically repeated by each of us when we go within to pray or meditate. Here, in this still, quiet place within the center of our being, we enter into the light of the spirit within. This is our inner connection with God and the true source of all life. We need to come here daily, renewing our direct contact with God, so we can keep our focus on the spirit within and not on the ego. The prayer for forgiveness on the Day of Atonement in the inner chamber of the temple simply represents what we each need to be doing every day in the inner chamber of our personal temple, where the living spirit resides.

(13) Jesus said to His disciples, "Compare me to someone and tell Me whom I am like." Simon Peter said to Him, "You are like a righteous angel." Matthew said to Him, "You are like a wise philosopher." Thomas said to Him, "Master, my mouth is wholly incapable of saying whom You are like." Jesus said, "I am not your master. Because you have drunk, you have become intoxicated from the bubbling spring which I have measured out." And He took him and withdrew and told him three things. When Thomas returned to his companions, they asked him, "What did Jesus say to you?" Thomas said to them, "If I tell you one of the things which He told me, you will pick up stones and throw them at me; a fire will come out of the stones and burn you up."

Teachers will monitor the progress of their students as they work their way through the material being presented. This usually comes in the form of a test, a quiz or a formal examination. Passing the test means the student has learned the material and is ready to progress to new material. For a spiritual teacher the general principle is the same but the nature of the material often does not lend itself to formal examinations. Spiritual growth is not like book learning: there generally are no facts, no mathematical formulas or stories to relate. What a true spiritual teacher is looking for is a change in perception and consciousness; more specifically, to what degree has this person's consciousness changed in relationship to the end goal of the Christ Consciousness?

"Compare me to someone and tell Me whom I am like" is a test of perception and consciousness. Simon Peter responds, "You are like a righteous angel." Matthew says, "You are like a wise philosopher." From these answers Jesus quickly sees that they are still functioning from the ego; the internal shift from ego to spirit has not yet taken place. Thomas answers, "Master, my mouth is wholly incapable of saying whom you are like." From this answer Jesus knows Thomas is no longer functioning from the ego; he no longer thinks in terms of the world. Thomas has recognized that there is something far beyond the usual things of the world at work within Jesus, but he has not progressed enough to clearly identify exactly what it is.

In the 1960's there was a popular song containing the phrase "First there is a mountain, then there is no mountain, then there is." This is a description of the general stages in this process of inner transformation. "First there is a mountain" recognizes the external structure of power and authority. As children, we are subject to the authority of our parents, teachers and others. As we become adults, we are still subject to others: our boss at work, law enforcement and other facets of the social structure. For most people this pattern of external power and authority does not change significantly. But for a person going through the inner transformation of spiritual growth the experience is quite different. The outer power structure is actually ego-based and ego-oriented. As the ego is dismantled through the process of self-discovery and self-examination, the external mountain of power and authority is dismantled along with it. We come to a place in our growth where "there is no mountain."

Having no mountain is a disorienting time. The usual guidelines of our worldly experience have lost their relevance; we are in essentially uncharted territory. This is where a true spiritual teacher makes all the difference. The teacher has been through the entire process before and can act as an effective guide along the journey to oneness with God and creation. This is where Thomas is; he has no mountain. The spirit within him has awakened and can now perceive the spiritual power and nature of Jesus, but he still lacks enough experience to put these perceptions in perspective. Thomas feels disoriented - lost. He sees, but he can't relate.

In the process of spiritual growth we gradually build a very personal relationship with God that is profoundly different from our worldly relationship. In the world, God is the ultimate power and authority figure - someone to be worshiped, feared and obeyed. It is similar in some respects to the relationship between parent and child. As we grow in the world and become parents ourselves, the relationship with our own parents changes. The love remains as does the respect, but the power and authority of the parent has dissolved. We relate more as two adults rather than parent and child. The same pattern is present in spiritual growth; we relate to God more as mature spiritual beings rather than parent and child. The basic structure is still there but the form of the relationship has changed.

The spiritual power and authority is rebuilt within instead of being outside of us. Now there is a mountain again; our perceptions have been placed within a new set of values and perspectives. Instead of the world as reference, the inner experience of the presence of God has become the reference for everything in our life. We have become spirit centered rather than ego centered. Our consciousness has been shifted from the temporary existence of the ego to the permanent existence of our spirit. We have crossed the bridge from death into eternal life. Separation has been left behind and we have entered into oneness.

Jesus tells Thomas, "I am not your master." The relationship has changed; Thomas is growing and in time he will mature and become like Jesus. Thomas has drunk from the bubbling spring of spirit and has become "intoxicated" – disoriented, the result of having no mountain. Thomas is now ready for more information, a deeper meaning, and a greater insight. Now Jesus can build on the level of understanding present in Thomas. The foundation of spiritual understanding has been laid and now the full structure of spiritual knowledge can be built. What Jesus tells Thomas is considered blasphemy by the outer form of religion, the penalty for which is being stoned to death.

Here is how it works between the outer form and the inner experience of religion. In the outer form you can believe, you can worship, but you can't become. In the inner experience there is only becoming. Jesus didn't ask us to worship him, he asked us to follow him - to become as he has become.

Thomas has learned that God is present in all things, even rocks and stones, and that God is not to be feared. But he has not yet learned that God is only love. There is still some ego left in Thomas for he still believes that God will harm others. He knows that he is safe, but he has not expanded that concept enough to include everyone.

(14) Jesus said to them, "If you fast, you will give rise to sin for yourselves; and if you pray, you will be condemned; and if you give alms, you will do harm to your spirits. When you go into any land and walk about in the districts, if they receive you, eat what they will set before you, and heal the sick among them. For what goes into your mouth will not defile you, but that which issues from your mouth – it is that which will defile you."

Here Jesus answers the questions asked by the disciples in saying (6). His answers highlight the difference between the inner and outer practices of religion. It is essentially a difference between form and substance. The outer practice of religion is one of form. For the disciples, the form is the Law of Moses, the 613 rules they learned in their Judaic faith. To sin is to fall short of the goal of keeping all of the rules. For one that has fallen short (sinned), there is a remedy that is used to atone for the short-coming. For minor sins, there was the sin offering, a sum of money paid to the temple or synagogue. For more serious sins, a more involved system of service to the temple or synagogue was performed. Everything was laid out in a concise system, a structure or framework which is recognized as the religion. The better people become at following the rules, the more religious they are.

The inner form taught by Jesus deals with substance rather than form. The rules are not only unimportant, but serve to stand in the way of actual inner transformation. The rules, the outer form of the religion, are primarily ego-based and keep the person centered in the ego and the experience of the outer world. This is why it works against inner transformation which must be spirit-centered. The practices of fasting, prayer and giving alms are not really the problem. Being ego-centered is the problem. By practicing the ego centered rules of the outer form of the religion the disciple moves away from the spirit, and this is why Jesus condemns the practice.

Jesus instructs his disciples, "When you go into any land and walk about in the districts, if they receive you, eat what they will set before you, and heal the sick among them." Doing so will result in breaking the rules of the outer form of religion, defiling the person by violating the dietary restrictions. But what the disciples are doing is being of real service to other people, the true children of God. This is the extension of the love that comes from God, flowing through us as it makes its way into the world. This is the activity of spirit: to help, to heal and to improve the general quality of life without adding a burden in the process. The ultimate action of the spirit is to liberate, not to oppress.

Jesus reminds his disciples that it is what comes out of their mouths that defiles them. What we say is a direct function of the things that are going on inside of us. Our thoughts, feelings, prejudices and attitudes are all reflected in the words we choose, the inflection of our voice, our body language and our actions. Just as some people will lie, some will seek to deceive using these modes of communication. But the truth will always come to the surface. People will eventually reveal their true inner selves. Then the substance of the inner-self will become clear. The ego will show itself with its ugly desires, or the spirit will shine with the light of God's pure love.

(15) Jesus said, "When you see one who was not born of woman, prostrate yourselves on your faces and worship him. That one is your Father."

All human bodies are born of woman. What is born of flesh is flesh, what is born of Spirit is spirit. It is the spirit within, the living light, the substance of God that gives us life. We are two things: a physical body, the gift of our earthly Mother, and a spirit, the gift of our heavenly Father. As we begin to "see" or perceive the spiritual being in each other, we begin to see the presence and substance of God. The term "worship" means "pay attention to". To prostrate ourselves on our faces is an act of total submission. So what Jesus is saying is that once we recognize the spirit within as the substance of God, we must pay attention to it; we must follow its lead and the ego must submit to its authority. This is the short version of spiritual growth.

One very important spiritual practice is to "see" or behold the Christ in each and every person. Once we have an intellectual understanding of the presence of spirit in everyone, we need to work on "getting a feel for it". This is how we "realize" or make something real. By repeating an act or perception we make it part of our consciousness. The goal is to shift our consciousness from the ego to the spirit, and recognizing the spiritual aspect of each and every person we encounter is an effective way of inducing this internal shift. As we practice "seeing" the spiritual person as well as the outer person, we eventually come to the point where one day we look in the mirror and we see the spirit within ourself. In essence, this is the point of the entire exercise: getting us to come face-to-face with the fact that we are spiritual beings – not just in theory, but in reality.

This is actually one of the disturbing realizations discussed in saying (2). Once the reality of our spiritual self begins to sink into our conscious mind, we are compelled to face the fact that almost everything we have been taught in the world may be wrong. A detailed, extensive self-inventory is required, and through this inner process of examining each of our assumptions and conclusions about ourself, each other, the world in which we live and our relationship with each other and God, we come to a new and unified perception of who and what we really are. We are then transformed from a human having a spiritual experience to a spiritual being having a human experience. The shift is profound. We have become spirit based rather than ego-based. We were lost, and now are found; blind, and now we see.

> **(16) Jesus said, "Men think, perhaps, that it is peace which I have come to cast upon the world. They do not know that it is dissension which I have come to cast upon the earth: fire, sword, and war. For there will be five in a house: three will be against two, and two against three, the father against the son, and the son against the father. And they will stand solitary."**

Family dynamics play an immense part in our development. We are subject to traumas, programming and imprinting within the family unit. These are the primary forces which shape our ego or personality. The results of these three forces determine the nature of our relationships and to a large degree help to determine our level of success in the world. Our self image and self worth are each forged by these three forces.

One of the primary goals in the process of spiritual growth is to overcome and replace the detrimental effects of the traumas, programming and imprinting which we have received as children. As this process begins, the family dynamics are examined and the conclusions we arrived at are re-evaluated. The basic problem is one of experience. We are thrust into an existing set of family dynamics even before we are born, being subject to the sounds and emotional state of the mother. Our birth also changes the family dynamics. We grow up in an environment over which we have little control, and due to our lack of experience, little understanding. Our mind seeks to make sense out of what is happening around us, and because we have no real base of experience and understanding, our conclusions are for the most part defective, incomplete, or just plain wrong. The classic example of this is the child deciding that the divorce of the parents is the child's fault.

The underlying principle is that the majority of our life decisions are based on assumptions and conclusions about life, relationships and ourselves which were made when we were children. If you want to see the impact this can have in your life, imagine a six-year-old making all of your decisions for you. As ridiculous as this may sound, it is not far from the truth. Our decisions as adults are formed around, and by, the perceptions we made as children. We come to conclusions and points of view at various times in our childhood, most of which never get reviewed in later adulthood. Our lack of experience and understanding in childhood becomes the formative factor in our perspectives and perceptions as adults. If we never re-examine the basis of our beliefs and actions, we never really mature.

Home is supposed to be a place of safety, refuge and peace, and yet it is the scene of private torment, conflict, and struggle for power and control. Family dynamics are generally anything but peaceful. When there are five in a house we generally think of two adults and three children. So the theme of two against three is generational: parents against the children. This premise is supported with the father against the son, and the son against the father. We must remember that this is an inner teaching; so while there are outer counterparts, the focus must remain on the inner experience. It is not the conflict in the family that we must resolve; it is the resulting inner conflict within each of us which is disrupting our lives that needs resolution. Indeed, once the inner conflict is resolved within the parents, the conflict within the family ceases.

This inner conflict is the direct result of the traumas, programming and imprinting which we received as children. It is necessary for us, as adults, to re-evaluate all of our assumptions and conclusions in life, bringing them into our full conscious awareness so we may see them for what they really are. Since traumas are the most destructive, we can reap the greatest benefits by working on them first. The fundamental factor is two-fold: first, some things just happen; accidents happen, people die, parents get divorced, careers are lost, and people become disabled. None of these things are directly attributable to us as a child. Life is not fair; it was never supposed to be fair. It is as it is. Second, many people will act out of their own pain, inflicting that pain on others. It is not necessary for you to have done something wrong; all you need to be is an available target. The classic statement of the persecutor is, "I wouldn't have to hurt you if you didn't make it necessary." It is the victim's fault that the persecutor is out of control.

People really are doing the best they can do, and yes, their best is sometimes extremely poor. The reality is that many people live their lives in turmoil and emotional pain, and their outer actions are but a reflection of that inner state. While we cannot change other people, we can change ourselves and we can establish a state of inner peace and serenity for ourselves. The process of spiritual growth involves the correction of past perceptions, conclusions, and emotional reactions. The correction is two-fold; the intellectual understanding must be changed, and the attached emotional state must also be changed. The key is to change both of them at the same time. We can use affirmations to change our thoughts, but if the emotional counterpart remains, the thought will be regenerated. We can change the emotional state, but if the intellectual counterpart (the conclusion) remains, the emotion will be regenerated. If we deal with both the intellectual and emotional sides at the same time then the resolution becomes permanent. Nothing remains to regenerate the other half.

The end result of this inner process is a unification of self, which is the "solitary" of which Jesus is speaking. The result is the complete surrender of the ego and its absorption into the authority of the spirit. As long as the ego remains, we are divided, living in a world of duality. Becoming spirit centered and dismantling the ego renders us solitary and able to enter into the oneness. It's all part of the same process of becoming one with God and all of creation. We will discuss this concept more in sayings 22, 23, 49, 55, 75, and 101.

(17) Jesus said, "I shall give you what no eye has seen and what no ear has heard and what no hand has touched and what has never occurred to the human mind."

The experience of the presence of God is so unlike anything else that people find they are unable to describe it. Our system of communication depends on common experiences. For example when I use the word "door", you know what a door is because you have experienced what a door does and what it does not do. It is this shared experience which allows us to communicate. Without that shared experience we lose our ability to communicate clearly. This is one of the reasons Jesus uses so many parables to describe the Kingdom of Heaven, or the Kingdom of God. Jesus is not trying to hide this experience or provide some cryptic explanation; he is trying to find some shared experience that can form a parallel with this experience of the presence of God. In this way, someone who has not experienced the presence of God may get an intellectual understanding of what the experience might be like.

No one has "seen", "heard" or "touched" the presence of God. It simply is not a thing of this world. As such, the human mind (ego or personality) has no idea what it is. This is not something that occurs to the human mind. If we really were "just human", then this experience could not happen to us. The fact that we can and do have this experience means that we are more than our bodies, more than our minds and thoughts. It is the presence of spirit within that not only allows, but also provides the mechanism through which this experience happens. In this way, experiencing the presence of God demonstrates the existence of spirit within each of us.

(18) The disciples said to Jesus, "Tell us how our end will be." Jesus said, "Have you discovered, then, the beginning, that you look for the end? For where the beginning is, there will the end be. Blessed is he who will take his place in the beginning; he will know the end and will not experience death."

People want to know what is going to happen to them. We want to know if there is a life after death, or if this is all there is. Jesus not only understands how life works, but also understands how the spirit works. The spirit exists first; it is the beginning. In the beginning was God, and from the substance of God we were produced. Nothing else in the universe needed to exist, just God, and then us. This is the beginning, the alpha. Physical life is a vehicle, a means of having the experiences we call life, a school where we can learn and grow into maturity. Once the need for the school has been met, we set the physical body aside; it is no longer needed. We take the lessons learned, the understanding and the wisdom with us. The mature spirit then has everything it needs; it is the omega, the end.

Once we make the shift from being ego-centered to being spirit-centered, we can shift our perceptions from the temporary nature of the body to the eternal nature of the spirit. By attaching our consciousness to the spirit, rather than the ego, we will not experience the death of consciousness. When the work of the body is done, we will set it aside; it will die, but our consciousness will not. We will continue on in full consciousness and awareness. In the Book of Revelation, where Jesus states he is the alpha and the omega, the beginning and the end, he is demonstrating that his consciousness is fully attached and associated with the spirit within. He is experiencing eternity here and now, and he is showing us how we can, too, by becoming spirit-centered and attaching our consciousness to our spirit instead of our ego.

(19) Jesus said, "Blessed is he who came into being before he came into being. If you become My disciples and listen to My words, these stones will minister to you. For there are five trees for you in Paradise which remain undisturbed summer and winter and whose leaves do not fall. Whoever becomes acquainted with them will not experience death."

In the traditional mystery school, the five trees are the Torah (the first five books of the Old Testament, the Torah being the original form written in Hebrew). By learning the spiritual system hidden within the Torah, we can make the shift from ego-centered to spirit-centered life and not experience death. While "Blessed is he who came into being before he came into being" may seem confusing, it refers to the spirit as described above. The comment of stones ministering to us will be addressed in saying #77.

The mystery school system was originally designed to impart the knowledge of spiritual existence, the raising up of the spirit to a position of power and authority in our life, bringing us fully and completely into that experience. It didn't take long for the remains of the ego to creep into the mystery school teachings and corrupt the pure spiritual essence of its message. The teaching soon was reserved for the elite, the socially and politically connected. The rest of humanity was considered "unclean" or "unwashed". The second meaning of "esoteric" then comes into play – meant for the few. The focus of the mystery school then moved from the practice of spiritual growth to the keeping of the knowledge or "secret".

In keeping this spiritual knowledge secret mankind has been relegated to a life of suffering without knowing why. Without the spiritual knowledge, the suffering of mankind cannot be overcome, so the suffering continues without end. Jesus recognized the inherent injustice in keeping the spiritual information secret and violated the order of secrecy. Jesus began teaching all who showed an interest and guided anyone, male or female, through the spiritual process and into the presence of God. This violation of secrecy led to his execution.

Jesus was not only teaching the secret knowledge, but also was teaching the practice of spiritual exercises designed to bring the presence of God into fruition. Knowledge without practical application is useless. The goal of this book is to share not only knowledge, but also practical methods so the information can be applied and the end result achieved. While the knowledge resides in the Torah, the practical method can be expressed in five other practices. Fulfilling our own inner needs opens the door to our spirituality. Those inner needs are: protecting our self, caring for our self, valuing our self, respecting our self and loving our self.

We have been trained to seek the fulfillment of those inner needs by manipulating the behavior of others, getting them to do these things for us. After all, how can you feel loved if there is no one there to love you? The reality is no one can make you feel loved, valued, cared for, respected or protected if you choose not to feel that way. Consider the man which falls madly in love with a woman. She has no attraction to, or desire to be with him. *Is* she loved? Yes! Does she *feel* loved? No! The man is a pest; she just wants him to go away. What we can learn from this is that even though we have learned to manipulate others, their action, and inevitable lack of action, is not going to fulfill our inner needs no matter what we do.

Let's look at another example. If we line up 100 people, and each person except one in the line tells us that we are a good person, who are we going to believe; the 99, or the one? Most of us are going to believe the one because they confirm the thoughts and feelings we have about ourselves. It is not about the views of other people, it is about the validation of what we think and feel about ourselves, and this internal reference controls how we feel, not the actions of another person. This is also what keeps us separated from God and all of creation.

Only by changing the internal reference, what we think and how we feel about ourselves, can we change our experience in life. It is up to us to develop respect for ourself, care about ourself, value ourself, protect ourself, and ultimately love ourself. Nothing else will work. Does this mean that we must become selfish? No, of course not. It means that we must stop manipulating other people and do for ourselves what needs to be done. We are responsible, not for the events in our lives, but for the effect those events have on us. We, not random or even intentional external events, determine what we think and how we feel. In taking responsibility for our thoughts and feelings, we remove a large part of the "mountain" that exists outside of us and move it within. We become the power and authority in our lives, not someone or something "out there".

At the same time, this moving of the power and authority from the outside to the inside does not mean we need to use that power to control another person; that's what got us into this problem in the first place. Power and authority are meant for each of us to control ourselves, not others. This is the power of autonomy – the power to control ourself. It is the ego which desires to control everything, but not itself. The spirit is into autonomy.

(20) The disciples said to Jesus, "Tell us what the Kingdom of Heaven is like." He said to them, "It is like a mustard seed, the smallest of all seeds. But when it falls on tilled soil, it produces a great plant and becomes a shelter for birds of the sky."

If we follow the interpretation of seeds as ideas, then creating the Kingdom of Heaven within is not looked on as one of the world's great ideas. Most people want something which does not require much work, yet provides substantial rewards. The work involved in spiritual growth is not difficult, but it requires persistence, a quality that involves continued activity with modest rewards along the way. The substantial reward attained through spiritual growth is cumulative; one experience or insight builds on another, moving us more and more into the ultimate experience of this 100% conscious contact with God.

The Kingdom of Heaven begins with a small idea, a simple concept. Oneness with God and all of creation is possible. The path begins with recognizing that we are separated from God not in reality, but in our mind and heart because we have held other things and ideas in greater esteem than the presence of God. The inner journey into the presence of God is the result of un-learning the past and re-learning the future. It involves a complete change in direction and purpose in life. This makes spiritual growth a daunting task, one which most people will not easily adopt. Just as the great plant that springs from the mustard seed does not appear overnight, so too does the Kingdom of Heaven grow slowly within.

Once the idea of the Kingdom of Heaven takes root in us and we start the process of un-learning and re-learning, the rest of our concepts begin to be altered. Soon the whole of our being is involved in the process. As we begin having spiritual experiences we get a taste of what the presence of God is really about. From that time on, we begin to hunger and thirst for these experiences and this intimate contact with God which comes to us. This is the hunger and thirst for righteousness of which Jesus speaks. Gradually, the spirit gains control of our lives and we are transformed into something much greater than we could have imagined. We express this greater self, not by ascending to a position of power and authority in the world, commanding millions of people, but in recognizing the spirit, the substance of God, in each and every individual we encounter. Our desire becomes one of service, in deep reverence and respect, clothed in kindness and gentleness. As such our compassion and humility become a welcome shelter for those around us. The greater our love, compassion and humility become, the greater the shelter we provide.

(21) Mary said to Jesus, "Whom are your disciples like?" He said, "They are like children who have settled in a field which is not theirs. When the owners of the field come they will say 'Let us have back our field.' They will strip themselves naked in their presence, in order to let them have their field and give it to them. Therefore I say unto you, if the master of the house knows that the thief is coming, he will begin his vigil before he comes and will not let him dig through into his house of his domain to carry away his goods. You then be on your guard against the world. Arm yourselves with great strength, lest the robbers find a way to come to you, for the difficulty which you expect will surely materialize. Let there be amongst you a man of understanding! When the grain ripened, he came quickly with his sickle in hand and he reaped. He who hath ears to hear let him hear."

While on the surface it may appear this saying is about four different things, when properly understood Jesus is talking about the same thing. The example Jesus uses of children who have settled in a field which is not theirs is representative of each of us in the early part of our spiritual journey. We have settled into a consciousness or belief system which is not secure. We don't "own" the experience yet. In the time of Jesus, children could not own land until they became adults. Even though the land may be theirs at some time in the future, someone else owns it until they are adults. Likewise, as we enter into a new belief system, we don't own the experience until we have matured enough to claim it and fully experience it for ourselves. Until then, when we are challenged by conditions in life, we revert to the old system of reactions that keep us limited and imprisoned. We quickly strip ourselves of the new ideas and concepts and return to our old trusted ways

Family and friends are usually the first to challenge us about our new beliefs. They have an interest in keeping us the same as we have always been. If we remain the same, or revert back to the same position, we validate what they believe about us and themselves. But if we change, then we are in effect challenging what others believe about themselves; questioning the status quo. This is why we are challenged in return: others feel threatened when we change, and the greater the change, the greater the challenge. Some people, when challenged in this way, abandon the new ideas and practices never to return. For those who persist, a change in beliefs also results in a change in friends and family relationships. Some will become closer, many will become more distant. It is all part of the process of growth.

Knowing that these challenges will come, we can prepare ourselves. "If the master of the house knows that the thief is coming, he will begin his vigil before he comes and will not let him dig through into his house of his domain to carry away his goods." So knowing that others will challenge our new ideas and concepts, we must begin preparing ourselves well in advance so we will not revert back into the old destructive patterns of thoughts, feelings and behaviors. We must not let the opinions of others add strength to the limiting and debilitating thoughts and feelings which we are trying to eliminate. We cannot allow others to continue validating the destructive patterns in our lives. We can do this by first limiting our time and associations with people who are not of like mind. Secondly, we can discount the comments these people make by understanding that they are acting out of their own pain, and not in consideration of us or our needs. We do not want them taking away our progress, "carrying away our goods."

"You then be on guard against the world. Arm yourselves with great strength, lest the robbers find a way to come to you, for the difficulty which you expect will surely materialize." This is the way the world works: when we challenge the status quo we are attacked to bring us back into line, back into submission. The old patterns of thought and belief are not easily replaced with the new. It is up to each of us to strengthen our resolve and protect the new ideas and practices until they take firm root in us, until we actually own the experience and become secure in our new consciousness.

"Let there be amongst you a man of understanding! When the grain ripened, he came quickly with his sickle in hand and he reaped." Inherent in this process is a matter of timing.

Like the parables of the fisherman and the pearl merchant, once we recognize that we have a workable path into the presence of God, we need to act. It does not take long for the world or our own ego to talk us out of doing what we need to do. Our interest strays and moves on to other things. In doing so, the opportunity to enter the Kingdom of Heaven passes and we remain in the world. If we clearly understand that the opportunity must be taken when it appears to us, just as grain must be harvested when it is ripe, then we will act and we will enter into the new consciousness.

> **(22) Jesus saw babes being suckled. He said to His disciples, "These babes being suckled are like those who will enter the Kingdom of Heaven." They said to Him, "Shall we then, as children, enter the Kingdom?" Jesus said to them, "When you make the two one, and when you make the inside as the outside and the outside as the inside and the above like the below and when you make the male and the female one and the same; so that the male shall not be male nor the female female; and when you fashion eyes in place of an eye, and a hand in place of a hand, and a foot in place of a foot, and an image in place of a likeness, then shall you enter the Kingdom of Heaven. He who hath a mind to understand, let him understand."**

The process of spiritual growth is one of transformation. This transformation involves the restructuring of everything within us. The primary work of restructuring is to unify our thoughts, feelings, actions and perspectives. The effect of the traumas, programming and imprinting creates a fractured nature within us. The mind attempts to coordinate and integrate the disparate experiences in our life, but finds it is unable to do so. What the mind does when it can't integrate is to compartmentalize. In order to maintain the illusion of integration, a device known as a buffer is created. The buffer is a momentary disorientation of the mind and thought pattern while our consciousness is switched from one compartment to another. Occasionally you will notice someone stating, "I never do anything like that" only to observe them doing just that 10 minutes later. This is the result of compartmentalization: one part does not know what the other part is doing.

When we become angry, we play out the actions and attitudes we have observed in others. We often use the same words, intonation and body language one of our parents used in the past. The power of imprinting is very strong. We are mostly unaware of its existence; let alone how deeply it has affected our life. All of the reactions we have to the many situations in life are the actions of one or more compartments, acquired through trauma, programming or imprinting. So very little of us is actually original, that once the personality is understood, our behavior can be predicted in advance to a very high degree of certainty. This is what profiling does and why it is used to help track down criminals. We really have become creatures of habit.

The transformative nature of spiritual growth identifies the individual compartments, breaks down the buffer, allowing us to "see" the true nature and source of this piece of our personality, and provides the means of integrating it into a new "whole". This is the underlying practice for what Jesus is describing. The end result of this process is a unified consciousness. We sometimes refer to such an individual as being "genuine", meaning they are the same in private as they are in public – there is no act which is put on to impress other people. This unification of self is necessary before we can enter into the Kingdom of Heaven.

(23) Jesus said, "I shall choose you, one out of a thousand, and two out of ten thousand, and they shall stand as a single one."

The process of inner unification begins when we select a central piece or perspective, into which all of the other pieces will be integrated. Since the goal and purpose is to awaken and empower the spirit within, and since the spirit is the only *real* or eternal part, the spirit is selected as the center of unification. When the spirit cannot be clearly identified, the spiritual part of the personality is selected to be replaced in the future as the true nature of the spirit within is revealed during the process of transformation.

(24) His disciples said to Him, "Show us the place where You are, since it is necessary for us to seek it." He said to them, "Whoever has ears, let him hear. There is light within a man of light, and he lights up the whole world. If he does not shine, he is darkness."

"Show us the place where you are" is a parallel to asking what the Kingdom of Heaven is like. We want to know what it will be like to consciously exist in the presence of God. The problem all spiritual teachers encounter is the lack of suitable words to describe an experience which is not shared by the vast majority of the population. This results in a wide variety of examples and explanations, most of which leave their students with more questions than when they started. Confusion is common. If it were a simple experience, it would be easier to explain. But the experience of the presence of God is a deeply moving one with many layers of subtlety, containing different aspects at the same time.

We have spoken of spirit as living light. This is more than a concept or an intellectual abstract. There is a physical reality to it. In the Book of Revelation 2:10 (RSV) Jesus says, "Be faithful unto death, and I will give you the crown of life." Many scholars have debated what this "crown" of life is. The most confusing aspect in the debate is the root word used for "crown". It is not a physical crown in the traditional sense. The Hebrew root word means "corona" as in the ring of light around the sun seen during a total solar eclipse. What relationship does this ring of light have to the crown, or highest expression, of life?

Spiritual growth is not just a change or elevation in consciousness; the spirit within us grows in size and power. We have more of the living light, more of the substance of God, and more of the life force. The divine spark becomes larger, much larger. As true spiritual mastery takes place, the living light of spirit becomes so strong that it is clearly visible, particularly around the head. This is exemplified by Moses in Exodus 34:30 (RSV), "And when Aaron and all the people of Israel saw Moses, behold, the skin of his face shone, and they were afraid to come near him." Many people now call this light a halo. A halo is an intensified form of the aura which appears around the head. Halos are represented in artwork of Jesus, some of the disciples, Mary Magdalene, and Mary, the mother of Jesus. These halos are not an invention of the imagination; they are the outward sign of true spiritual mastery. There is much more going on in the history of these religious figures than we have been led to believe.

The living light of spirit is real and a true spiritual master does shine. The living light of spirit shines in a halo around the head, like the corona around the sun. This is the highest expression of spiritual power on earth; it is the highest level of the life force, the crown of life.

(25) Jesus said, "Love your brother like your soul, guard him like the pupil of your eye."

There is a profound connection between love and the spirit. Jesus gave us a new commandment: that we love one another. The reason for this new commandment is not just something which would be nice to do; it is the essence of the spiritual growth processes. It is love which awakens the spirit and soul. It is love which empowers the living light within. It is love which is the mechanism of inner transformation. Without feeling this love that comes from God we cannot experience the presence of God, for the two are one and the same.

As we enter more deeply into the presence of God, the love which comes from God becomes stronger, flowing through us, radiating from us out into the world. We are changed at depth through the experience of love. It is extending to others the love we feel and experience, which creates the flow through us. It is like the flow of water in a stream or river; if it is not flowing there is no power to it. Love is the same way – no flow, no power. If this love is not flowing through us, we cannot experience it, either. We cannot hang on to it; either it flows, blessing us and making us grow in the process, or we don't experience it at all. To love our brother like our soul is to assist the flow of love through us. To guard him like the pupil of our eye is to prevent anything from interfering with that flow of love.

(26) Jesus said, "You see the mote in your brother's eye, but you do not see the beam in your own eye. When you cast the beam out of your own eye, then you will see clearly to pull the mote from your brother's eye."

The ego looks out into the world and judges it good or bad. It has no incentive to examine itself, for the one who judges must always be superior to what is being judged. In the process of judging others it is easy to find fault, diminishing the value of anyone who would compete against us in the world.

The spiritual path is the journey of self discovery. This entails the exploration of all of our inner qualities, faults included, with the intent of resolving all of our inner conflicts. This process leads to the unification of the self and removes the blocks to our awareness and clears our perceptions. It is only when we see others through the eyes of the love which comes from God that we see them clearly, the way God sees them. Only then are we truly in a position to help them. How can we give something which we do not have? How can we guide someone on a path we are not walking? The simple reality is that we cannot. Our growth must be well along in its progress before we can guide others. We must be well established in love before we see others as true children of God. Before we can show others what we really are, we must become our real self.

(27) Jesus said, "If you do not fast as regards the world, you will not find the Kingdom. If you do not regard the Sabbath as Sabbath, you will not see the Father."

There is a story about a Cherokee elder who was teaching his grandchildren about life. He said to them, "A fight is going on inside me. It is a terrible fight between two wolves. One wolf represents fear, anger, envy, sorrow, regret, greed, arrogance, self-pity, guilt, resentment, inferiority, lies, pride and superiority. The other wolf stands for joy, peace, love, hope, sharing, serenity, humility, kindness, benevolence, friendship, empathy, generosity, truth, compassion and faith. This same fight is going on inside of you and every other person too." The grandchildren thought about it for a minute and then one child asked; "Grandfather, which wolf will win?" The old man simply replied, "The one I feed."

Within us are two competing entities: the ego and the spirit. In our early development, we associate with the ego, and it is the ego which gets fed. As a result the ego grows in strength and power. As long as it gets fed, the ego is in control of our life. So what are we actually doing that feeds our ego?

We have come to know that we eat food, drink water, and breathe air, and our bodies use these basic components to create the energy we need to move our muscles and do the physical and mental activities which fill our days. What we don't know is that the body is a biological energy transformation machine. It is capable of creating a number of different specific forms of energy, not just the form needed by the muscles, organs and brain. The body produces a form of emotional energy which matches the energy requirements of the ego. This form of emotion is fear or pride-based and is something we normally associate with negative emotions. Fear, hate, anger, guilt, envy, bitterness, resentment, lust and shame are emotions in this class. These are the emotions which feed the ego. Every time we express or experience these emotions the ego is being fed, becoming stronger and more in control of our lives.

The spirit needs a different form of energy than the ego. The spirit feeds on the positive emotions of love, compassion, caring, gentleness, kindness, respect and support. The crux of the issue is that the body will produce only one of these forms at a time. As we have spent most of our life experiencing the emotions which feed the ego, the ego has grown very strong. The spirit, which has not been fed, has lapsed into a deep sleep, like a state of hibernation. This is where the concept of awakening applies to the spirit. We must awaken the spirit from its deep sleep before it can be raised up and empowered. So how do we awaken our spirit? We start feeding it. We make a conscious decision and effort to experience only positive, loving emotions.

Is this a practical approach? Well, yes and no. Will experiencing positive emotions awaken the spirit? Yes. Can we just switch from negative to positive emotions by choosing to do so? No. Our ego has a very strong interest in keeping us focused on the emotions which feed it. Without that food, the ego will weaken and eventually fall into a deep sleep, just as our spirit has. This is the fight between the "two wolves" within us, the ego and the spirit. We decide which will win, by deciding which we will feed. And we feed one or the other by the emotions we express and experience. Do not be discouraged when the ego raises its ugly head and you are thrown back into a negative emotion. The answer is in being persistent. Return to the loving emotions as soon as you can. The more love-based emotions you can experience, the more the spirit within you will grow; and the stronger the spirit becomes, the more loving thoughts and emotions you will experience.

The world runs on negative emotions. A simple review of the day's news makes that clear. As long as we indulge in the emotions which feed the ego, the spirit within cannot grow. We must stop our indulgence in the negative emotions; we must fast as regards the world and stop feeding the ego. If we do not stop feeding the ego, the spirit will not grow and we cannot find the Kingdom. It's that simple.

The Sabbath is the traditional day of rest. Here the rest Jesus is referring to is the same as in saying #2 (Coptic version). Rest represents the peace of God, that deep abiding peace which is the hallmark of living in the presence of God. Rest is also associated with the practice of meditation, the traditional means of entering into the presence of God for many Eastern religions. Here the practice focuses on quieting the mind and bringing it into a state of peace. The key to successful spiritual growth through meditation is the same as any other spiritual system: confronting and resolving the disturbances within the personality or ego. If there is no inner confrontation followed by resolution, there is no growth.

(28) Jesus said, "I take my place in the midst of the world, and I appeared to them in the flesh. I found them all intoxicated; I found none of them thirsty. And My soul became afflicted for the sons of men, because they are blind in their hearts and do not have sight. For empty they came into the world, and empty too they seek to leave the world. But for the moment they are intoxicated. When they shake off their wine, then they will repent."

The world has seen a great procession of spiritual teachers. These teachers come into the world, taking their place, appearing in the flesh so they are like everyone else. Then they demonstrate their spiritual knowledge and understanding, showing others the way back into the presence of God. But life in the world has its own way. By having life in the world structured to focus on and feed the ego, we become entranced with the ego's desires, thoughts and goals. We are led to believe the ego is all there is, and either you get with the program and become the biggest ego around, or you're nobody. The ego blinds us by making its focus the outside rather than the inside. The ego is calling us to go out into the world and find our answers "somewhere out there".

The spiritual teacher calls us back to the inner world of spirit where the presence of God can be found. The problem all spiritual teachers encounter is the entranced state of people living under control of the ego. Jesus describes this entranced state as being intoxicated. He states he found none of them thirsty. In other words, none of them is seeking true knowledge and understanding of spiritual things. There is no hunger and thirst for righteousness, living a spirit-based life in the presence of God. All true spiritual teachers grieve for the suffering people experience. The most frustrating part is seeing how the thoughts, feelings and actions of people create that suffering. People do not see how the ego manipulates them into emotional pain and suffering, just so it can get fed. The stronger the ego becomes the more suffering it creates, either within the self, or in other people.

Each person is a spiritual being, but without the fullness and depth of that experience, we are empty and desolate. Without the spiritual teacher there would be no effective way of ending the separation from God and the suffering that ensues from that separation. There is an old story about a wolf and a flock of sheep. The wolf is having trouble catching the sheep because the entire flock is very much aware of the wolf and what the wolf wants. So the flock avoids the wolf, keeping its distance. The wolf thinks and thinks and finally comes up with a plan. The wolf hypnotizes the flock and tells them they are no longer sheep. He tells each sheep, "You are a doctor, you are a teacher, you are an engineer and you are a lawyer." As the sheep go about believing they are these other things, they forget their real nature and the threat the wolf is to them. The wolf can now approach the sheep and kill whichever one it wants without the sheep becoming alarmed.

In this story the wolf represents our ego. The ego keeps its victims entranced, hypnotized or intoxicated, so they do not clearly see what it is doing to them. The spiritual teacher shakes the belief system and attempts to awaken or bring the student out of the trance or hypnotized state induced by the ego. Generally only the few will shake off this intoxication of the ego and repent. The meaning of the word "repent" is not only an act of contrition, but the changing of one's mind, and just as importantly, to change ones life. To repent is to change the direction of one's life: from outer to inner, from ego to spirit, from separation to oneness.

This is the call which every true spiritual teacher makes: repent. Change your thoughts, your feelings and your actions. Turn away from the ego and its incessant focus on suffering, manipulation and control. Change your life by changing your consciousness. The presence of God is everywhere, in and of everything, at all times. It is only our state of consciousness which limits our awareness, and we can change that. We can grow in awareness, knowledge, understanding and wisdom. We can awaken the spirit within, grow and mature into the pure spiritual being God created us to be. We are limited only by our lack of understanding who and what we really are. You are a child of God, created out of God substance. Everything God is and has is yours.

(29) Jesus said, "If the flesh came into being because of spirit, it is a wonder. But if the spirit came into being because of the body, it is a wonder of wonders. Indeed, I am amazed at how this great wealth has made its home in this poverty."

The Spirit which we recognize as God is the source of all life. The individualized substance of God which we recognize as our own personal spirit is the source of our individual life. The spirit is present and forms a living light field around the sperm and egg just before conception takes place. The genetic DNA of the new body is formed during conception, becoming the blueprint for the body. So how does a cell know what it is to become? In the beginning individual cells are undifferentiated; they are not bone cells, muscle cells, skin cells or nerve cells. How does a cell know it has to become a bone cell for example? We might say the DNA within the cell makes that determination based on where the cell is in the developing body. But the question still remains: *how* does it know? How does the cell "know" where it is in the newly forming body?

DNA does not "think", therefore it cannot "know"; DNA is a repository for information, much like a library full of books. Just as a library requires someone to read the books and understand them before the information can be used and become meaningful, so too must the DNA be read and understood before it can be used in a meaningful way. So who or what "reads" the DNA? It is this author's belief that the spirit within us "reads" the DNA and supervises the construction of the physical body, following the blueprint created during conception.

On a more philosophical level, the individual spirit needs the physical body for its development and maturing process. The body is a biological energy transformation system capable of producing the specific form of energy needed by the spirit for its growth. So the flesh (the body) comes into being because of the spirit. The spirit, being the substance of God, has eternal life. It has come into existence from pure Spirit, not physical matter. God has existed from before the creation of the physical universe. The creator must exist before the creation as a matter of definition of terms. Just as God is the creator of the physical universe, so too are we as spiritual beings the creator of our physical bodies. The creator gives rise to the creation, not the other way around. This is why Jesus says, "But if the spirit came into being because of the body, it is a wonder of wonders." It just doesn't work that way.

What is amazing is that the spirit, with its great wealth of possibilities, ultimately inheriting the full Kingdom of God, has chosen the limited nature of the physical body for its temporary home. The key to understanding this choice is the capability of the physical body to generate the specific form of energy required for the spirit to grow. Without this energy, the spirit cannot develop beyond where it currently exists. The undeveloped spirit is also without full consciousness and awareness. These, too, are developed during this partnership with the physical body. So the body is an instrumental tool in the development of the spirit.

(30) Jesus said, "Where there are three gods, they are gods. Where there are two or one, I am with him."

Here is the Greek version.

(30) [Jesus sa]id, ["Wh]ere there are [th]r[ee] t[hey ar]e [without] God. And [w]here there is only o[ne], I say, I am with hi[m]. Li[f]t the stone and there you will find me. Split the wood and I am there."

The Greek version combines part of saying #77 which we will save for that explanation. It is obvious the first line is at odds in these two translations, so we will begin with the Greek version. Always remember esoteric teachings or sayings deal with inner things, even though they are expressed in outer terms. "Where there are three they are without God" would be more clear if it said "where there are three *or more* they are without God."

There is an old story about a man who desires to lead a spiritual life. His wife has died and his children are grown so he comes to the temple and asks to enter the spiritual life of a monk. A teacher at the temple tells him first he must attend classes which are held once a week outside the entrance to the temple. So the man starts to attend the classes. After about a year he comes into the temple and begins explaining to the master of the temple how he wants to lead a spiritual life and live with them in the temple. The master interrupts saying, "Stop, stop, there are too many voices. Go back to class."

After returning to class the man begins to pay close attention to anything having to do with voices. He discovers he says some of the same things his father said when he was a boy, and he asks the teacher if this is what is meant by voices. The teacher explains that this is exactly what the master of the temple was talking about. Within us are many voices which we have incorporated over the years, and it is necessary for us to separate these voices and eliminate all voices except the one true voice which is our real self. After another year of work on voices the man approaches the master of the temple again and tries to explain what he wants. The master again interrupts saying, "Stop, stop, there are still too many voices. Go back to class."

Now the man knows he is on the right track. He discovers he says things his mother used to say, his childhood friends, his uncle, his aunt, his grandfather, his teachers at school, his boss where he worked; all of them have had an impact on him and all have taken a place within his mind. He began to ask himself, "Who am I, really?" One by one he began to identify and discard the patterns of speech, the mannerisms, the attitudes and prejudices of the people in his life. Finally the day came when he felt he was ready to approach the master again. This time when he entered the temple he simply went and stood in front of the master and said nothing. The master looked deeply into his eyes and studied him for several minutes. Finally the master said, "Not perfect, but better. Now we can begin."

Within each of us reside the voices, the attitudes and beliefs of others. We are not just ourselves, we are a mixture of ourself and many others, each part separate from the others. We are not unified. God will not enter the crowded room. Only where we have reduced the voices within to one or two will the spirit and oneness of God enter. As long as there are three or more voices, they rule our consciousness and control our lives. The voices have become our Gods. Where there are three or more voices, they are (false) Gods. Where there are two or one, the true spirit and oneness of God can enter.

(31) Jesus said, "No prophet is accepted in his own village; no physician heals those who know him."

Our belief about people is one of the strongest factors in the construction of relationships. When we grow up knowing someone we tend to think this is the way they will always be. But people change. The maturing process changes people more than anything else in our society. As we mature in the world we cease to be the children we have been; we in essence become a new person.

Part of the problem is that physical maturity is automatic but the rest of our maturity requires effort on our part. Intellectual, emotional and spiritual maturity is not automatic. Intellectual maturity requires us to learn and put what we learn to use. Emotional maturity is more involved. This involves sometimes painful changes and the releasing of immature emotional states and actions. A lack of emotional maturity severely limits many people in their careers and relationships. The vast majority of relationship difficulties are the result of emotional immaturity. Whether it takes place at home or at work, the pain and suffering and loss of productive time and effort represent tremendous losses for us all. It's not just the economic loss but the loss of loving, caring relationships resulting in damaged and dysfunctional families. This creates very deep seated painful emotional traumas that warp and twist our personalities, perpetuating the emotional harm for generations.

Ignorance is addressed through education, but how do we address the lack of emotional maturity in our society? Generally, we don't. Our society is struggling to meet simple goals of basic education. Learning about emotional maturity is far beyond what we currently can conceive as a society. Some individuals have seen the need and are trying to raise awareness about our emotional states, but at this time it exceeds the grasp of our society. If emotional maturity is beyond our grasp, spiritual maturity is beyond our comprehension.

For this reason, the rare individual who manages to mature spiritually is considered a prophet. People who have known this person before the maturing process has taken place still think they know them, and they certainly can't be anything other than what they were. People always assume that the most spiritual people have to be from somewhere else; there can't be any prophet here, because I know everybody from here. What is not understood is that everyone is a spiritual being living the life of a regular person. Anyone who has the desire and knowledge can grow emotionally and spiritually.

We tend to think that these rare spiritually matured people are going to be so different from us that we would instantly recognize them. So what would we look for? Walking on water or performing miracles? That would certainly make the recognition easy, but real life is not so simple. You may already know a spiritually mature person. The most obvious outer signs are treating everyone with respect, gentleness and kindness. Spiritually mature people are peaceful, generally happy and non-confrontational. There is an inner joy and truly loving nature about them. People find that they like the spiritually mature person, often without knowing why. Spiritually mature people stand out, but in ways which we don't normally expect. When we meet them for the first time we clearly recognize that something is very different about them, but if we have known them for years, our past perceptions about them blind us to their current level of maturity.

(32) Jesus said, "A city being built on a high mountain and fortified cannot fall, nor can it be hidden."

Spiritually mature people are different, and the greater the maturity the greater the difference. A city being built on a high mountain is the consciousness being built on the base of spirit rather than ego. As in saying #21, it takes time and effort to build this new consciousness. At some point the new consciousness becomes strong enough to withstand the criticism from others in the world which results from becoming spiritually mature and thus different. The desire to conform is strong in most people and it takes a certain degree of spiritual maturity to overcome the need to conform. Once the new consciousness has been strengthened and fortified, it becomes secure; it will not fall. But it is also at this point that it cannot be hidden, either. The change from being ego-based to being spirit-based becomes obvious.

(33) Jesus said, "Preach from your housetops that which you will hear in your ear and in your other ear. For no one lights a lamp and sets it under a bushel, nor does he put it in a hidden place, but rather he sets it on a lampstand so that everyone who enters and leaves will see its light."

The new consciousness brings with it more insights into the nature of God. These insights, or revelations, can be exciting. We want to tell others about what is happening to us and what we are learning. We are sometimes dismayed that other people are not receptive to our new-found experiences. We forget about the disillusionment we experienced in the earlier part of our spiritual journey (saying #2). By remembering, we can see how the new ideas can be disruptive to the belief systems of other people.

As we grow and mature spiritually the lamp of enlightenment becomes lit within us. Although some people enter temples or monasteries to get out of the world and into their own spiritual environment, it is not appropriate to go into seclusion and hide from the world. We must live our lives, letting the light of spirit shine through our kindness, gentleness, and loving respect for others. Through our actions more than words we express the loving nature of the Kingdom of Heaven, touching the minds and hearts of those around us. The light within will shine, and we must allow it to do so.

(34) Jesus said, "If a blind man leads a blind man, they will both fall into a pit."

As we have discovered in the Gospel of John, chapter 3, the ego cannot see the Kingdom of Heaven. It is only the spirit within which has the capability to perceive the Kingdom. In this respect, anyone who is ego based is blind to the Kingdom. This is the underlying difference between the outer form of religion and the inner experience. The outer form must rely on the ego which can only believe and have faith. The inner form sees and experiences the Kingdom, and thus "knows" (gnosis). The ego can go on a spiritual path, but it is blind to the Kingdom and must lose its way. Those following an ego on a spiritual path must also lose their way.

It doesn't matter what the ego learns, for if our consciousness is attached to the ego it will all disappear once the body can no longer produce the energy needed to sustain the ego. The result is the second death spoken of in the Book of Revelation (20:14 & 21:8): the death of consciousness. The Book of Revelation presents this as a lake of fire which destroys everything thrown into it. The pit Jesus uses in this example is another metaphor with the same meaning and function. The pit is the darkness which results from the loss of consciousness.

(35) Jesus said, "`It is not possible for anyone to enter the house of a strong man and take it by force unless he binds his hands; then he will be able to plunder his house."

The ego does not surrender easily. When we begin our true spiritual path the ego is strong. It is necessary to bind the hands of the ego so we can empty ourselves of the traumas, programming and imprinting. These are the things the ego uses as tools or weapons in maintaining control over our lives.

In many ways the ego is like a small child; it likes to misbehave, but it doesn't like to get caught. So we "bind its hands" by observing the ego. We then "catch" the ego doing what it does to control us. In order to accomplish this, we need to learn something about how the ego works. The ego is subject to triggers, both external and internal. An external trigger is an event which happens outside of us. It can be something someone says or does. It can be the tone of someone's voice or someone's body language. It can be a sound, smell, texture, color, taste; anything which triggers a memory within us. An internal trigger is a memory, usually of an external trigger. It doesn't matter whether the trigger is internal or external because once the process has been triggered, the rest of it is all internal.

Many triggers are pleasant to most of us: the smell of coffee or of freshly baked bread, fresh cut flowers, a thank you note. These generally invoke pleasant memories from our past. But some triggers invoke feelings of guilt, anger, frustration, hatred, envy and a host of other negative feelings and their associated thoughts. There is a sequence which follows the trigger. The first is a feeling. Feelings are faster than thoughts. In a sequence, feelings and thoughts are connected. The first feeling is not usually very strong, but it is connected to a thought, generally a conclusion we have come to about ourself, someone else, life, or our perception of the relationships involved. The thought acts as an internal trigger, activating a second emotion which is related to the first feeling and acts as support for the developing emotional experience.

A type of ping-pong ball exchange follows where the feeling is attached to a thought, which acts as an internal trigger for the next related feeling. The end effect is the building of an emotional state within, generally negative in nature, where the ego can gorge itself on the emotional energy produced. The disruptive consequences to the rest of our life and the lives of others around us are ignored, at least for the moment. If the action of the ego has injured someone physically or emotionally, guilt can always be served as desert; any negative or pride based emotion will feed the ego. What we are looking for is the ping-pong ball game, the sequence of feelings and thoughts which are used to build the negative emotional state.

Keep a small pad or notebook handy for writing down your observations. In the beginning it is common to go through the entire emotional sequence before we realize we should have been observing. Persistence is the key. Don't beat yourself up for missing what happened; that can be used to feed the ego, as well. Just continue to observe how emotional states are generated. Make a list of emotions which are triggered within you and their associated thoughts. Many times the ego will indulge in these emotional feasts when you can't write them down, for example, while you are driving a car or are in the middle of doing something which cannot be interrupted. As soon afterwards as you can, write down as much of the feeling / thought pattern as you can remember.

After about a month of observation you should begin to recognize a pattern developing in the feeling / thought ping-pong game. There will be three or four emotional states which the ego uses to feed itself. As you become more adept at observing, you will begin to see the triggers which initiate the emotional states. Once you recognize the triggers you can begin to watch for them. The negative emotional state can be avoided by breaking the ping-pong ball sequence, and the earlier in the sequence we can break the pattern the less the ego gets fed. Not feeding the ego makes it weak. This is how we bind the hands of the strong man (the ego), so we can plunder his house (take away the tools or weapons the ego has been using against us).

(36) Jesus said, "Do not be concerned from early until late and from evening until morning about food, what you shall eat, nor about clothing what you shall put on. Much better are you than the lilies, which card not neither do they spin, and your Heavenly Father clothes them also. For who can defile you? Who can add to your age? He Himself will give you your garment."

Historically the Essenes and many other related religious groups were communal in nature. This means that they shared resources; there was no private property. In exchange for their labor, individuals were supplied with food, clothing and shelter in addition to spiritual instruction. We live in a different way now, so the outer experience is different. But the inner experience is still the same. It has to do with the focus in our life. Remember, worship means "pay attention to". The things we pay attention to in our life are the subject of our worship. So what are we paying attention to? What are we worshiping?

Are we focused on food, clothing, appearance or possessions? If we have no food, clothing or shelter, it is necessary to focus on them, for the physical body we inhabit requires those things for survival. But beyond the basics, what do we really need? Conveniences like washing machines, dryers, refrigerators, freezers, cars for transportation, TV's and radios for communication and entertainment and furniture to sit and lie on are all good things to have. But somewhere there is a line between what is needed and useful and what is possessed for the impression it makes on other people. This is why focus is so important. Are we focusing on our survival and basic comfort, or are we focusing on elevating our ego and creating separation between ourselves and others, if only in our mind?

If we are to mature emotionally and spiritually, we must focus our attention on the things which will heal the separation and bring us into oneness. Who can defile us? The ego defiles us. Remember it is not that which goes into the mouth, but that which proceeds from the mouth which defiles us. For what we say reflects what is in our heart. The ego acts in its own interest, out of our lower (negative) emotional base. This defiles us. The spirit acts in the interest of oneness and healing, out of our higher, love-based, emotional center. This blesses us and also blesses all others with whom we come in contact. The ego acts to increase the separation, thus increasing the pain and suffering it inflicts on the world. The spirit acts to heal the separation and bring us into oneness, thus reducing the pain and suffering in the world. This is the power of focus. This is why our focus is so important. Reducing the suffering in the world is an altruistic goal which may have little real meaning to us in our everyday life. But reducing the suffering we experience individually is much more rewarding and beneficial to us on a personal level. Suffering is suffering, and if you stop suffering there is less suffering in the world, is there not?

He himself will give you your garment. We are also clothed in our attitude and consciousness. What difference does it make if people are dressed in expensive clothes when they are rude and abusive? Clothing does not change who they are. As we enter into the presence of God and begin functioning from gentleness, kindness and respect, we become clothed in love. It is by our loving nature that people recognize us, not by our clothing. Are we to be people of inner substance or remain shallow, without character and depth to our being? Living in the presence of God is the single most powerful and transforming experience in life. You cannot go through that experience and not become a beautiful person within.

(37) His disciples said to him, "When shall you be revealed to us and when shall we see You?" Jesus said, "When you strip yourselves without being ashamed, and take up your garments and place them under your feet like little children and tread on them, then will you see the Son of the Living One, and you will not be afraid."

"When shall you be revealed to us and when shall we see You?" Notice the use of upper case and lower case in the two uses of the word "you". Just as in spirit and Spirit, we are talking about two different levels of experience, the individual and the divine. It is difficult for the ego to determine who is a true spiritual teacher and who is just another ego on a spiritual path. So the disciple's question is what the ego part of us really wants to know. The ego wants proof of a person's spiritual development. If this developed spirit is inside of you, show it to me.

Unless a person is adept at seeing auras and understands what they are seeing, the ego remains without eyes to see. The ego cannot see the Kingdom of Heaven; only the spirit within can perceive these spiritual things. Jesus understands their desire for proof of spiritual attainment; the disciples want to see the raised-up spiritual being – the "You" in question. The disciples cannot see the spiritual being within in their present state of consciousness. So Jesus tells them what they must do in order to enter into the consciousness which will allow them to see. "When you strip yourselves without being ashamed, and take up your garments and place them under your feet like little children and tread on them" refers not to actual clothing, but to the ego-based consciousness and the attitudes and acts we put on for the impression it will make on others. We feel ashamed of the person we really are, so we put on this act, this persona, when we are out in public. It is only at home where we let down the appearances and start to be ourself.

In the process of spiritual growth the acts, the public persona, the need to make favorable impressions gradually fall by the wayside. They lose their importance as the spirit begins to be awakened and raised-up to a position of power and authority in our lives. Treading on something is a show of disrespect. When we come to the point where we disrespect the ego and everything it has to offer, we are well into the process of transferring our consciousness from the ego to the spirit within. It is at this point we begin to see the raised-up spirit clearly. "Then you will see the Son of the Living One, and you will not be afraid." Again, notice the use of upper case letters on "Son" and "Living One". "Son" refers to the awakened and raised-up spirit within. "Living One" is another way of saying the spiritual aspect of God. Spirit is the source of all life and the "Living One" is another way of recognizing that source.

We have been well trained to view God in fear. But our direct experiences with the presence of God gradually teach us there is nothing to fear. By the time we grow sufficiently to see the spiritual being within we will have lost our fear of God.

(38) Jesus said, "Many times have you desired to hear these words which I speak to you and have had no one else to hear them from. There will be days when you shall seek Me, and will not find Me."

The opportunity to learn from a fully awakened teacher is rare. Many times we may imagine what it would be like to listen to such a teacher. But our ability to understand is limited by our consciousness, so we may not perceive what is really being said to us. The true spiritual teacher makes every effort to communicate clearly, knowing concepts and explanations will have to be repeated a number of times before they really begin to sink in. There is a window of opportunity for learning spiritual principles and inner truths before the ego loses interest and returns to the concerns of the world. Life moves on and so do spiritual teachers. When the opportunity for spiritual growth comes to you, take it; do not delay.

(39) Jesus said, "The Pharisees and the scribes have taken the keys of Knowledge and hidden them. They themselves have not entered, nor have they allowed to enter those who wish to. You, however, be as wise as serpents and as innocent as doves."

The mystery school system was originally founded to bring spiritual truths to mankind. People were screened for their readiness and ability to understand the information being presented. As happens with all religious systems, eventually people with active egos find their way into positions of authority and the original purpose becomes corrupted. By the time of

Jesus, the mystery school system had evolved into a private club for the elite and politically and socially connected. The actual teaching of practice and spiritual growth and development of the spirit within had given way to the protection of "secret" knowledge. It simply became one more way for people to separate themselves from one another. The screening for suitable students had shifted from ability to position in society.

The Pharisees and the scribes became the keepers of the "secret" knowledge. Because the system was now ego-based, there was no real interest in practice and becoming; just in keeping the "secret". Jesus was of royal birth, and as such, was granted entry into the mystery school system. Upon completing the highest initiation and learning the most secret information, Jesus realized that the secret information was simply a key to understanding how to awaken, raise, and empower the spirit within. The real secret wasn't the information itself, but the system of practices, or the process, which leads to spiritual maturity. So in addition to the secret information, Jesus began teaching the practices needed for spiritual growth. His teaching of forgiveness was a key element of the process for spiritual awakening and growth.

The mystery school system taught a well-rounded system of knowledge in addition to spiritual information. Mathematics, the sciences, arts and philosophy were all part of the knowledge base offered by the schools. As in many of the past centuries, there was little education outside of religious establishments. To become educated meant becoming part of the religious system. To be wise as serpents involved entering and learning the knowledge taught in the mystery school system, which used the serpent as its symbol, and a sign of its graduates. To be innocent as doves was to shed the ego and the false pretenses of societal position and power - something the usual graduates of the mystery school system did not do. The gateway to power and influence in the time of Jesus was through the mystery school system and its club of influential patrons.

Jesus had a different agenda for his students. Learn the information the system has to offer, but do not get caught up in the politics and intrigue. Use the knowledge for real spiritual growth so you can set yourself free from the world and its entrapments. The knowledge provides the key; the practice provides the means of inner transformation. Here is the single most important key to understanding spiritual sayings, principles and parables. It is always about consciousness.

(40) Jesus said, "A grapevine has been planted outside of the Father, but being unsound, it will be pulled up by the roots and destroyed."

The grapevine is the ego. It has been created outside of the Father, outside of the realm of spirit. It is unsound because it is temporary; once the body is gone the energy system which supports the ego is also gone. The ego will gradually weaken and fade from existence. When it does, whatever consciousness has been attached to the ego dies with it.

If we are to move our consciousness from the ego over to the spirit, the ego must be dismantled - pulled up by the roots and destroyed. This is exactly what the practice and process of spiritual growth accomplishes. The ego is not actually totally destroyed. For in the end it recognizes its proper place and surrenders completely to the will of spirit: thy will be done, not mine. But for all practical purposes, the process carries on with the goal of destroying the ego.

Some have identified this practice with a form of nihilism, a doctrine advocating that all things are worthless and unknowable. This is not correct for things in the world do have some value. The Gnostic teachings of Jesus also insist that all things are knowable; nothing will remain hidden. If you see the ego as the only thing which exists within, then the spiritual growth practice could appear threatening. Even those who follow a path of eliminating all attachments to things of the world find that they end up with everything, not nothing.

(41) Jesus said, "Whoever has something in his hand will receive more, and whoever has nothing will be deprived even of the little that he has."

This is the parallel to the parable of the talents. In Matthew 25:14-30 (RSV) talents are given the servants; five to one, two to another and one to a third. A talent is a measurement of weight, about 75 pounds. In money, this would be something very valuable. The master returns and demands an accounting of what has been done with the talents given to the servants. The ones with five and two talents have each doubled what they were given. These are rewarded and told "Well done, good and faithful servant; you have been faithful over a little, I will set you over much; enter into the joy of your master." The one servant, however, buried the talent, returning it in its original condition. This servant is punished, and what little he has is taken from him and given to those who have more.

The inner spiritual meaning is that we are each given something of great value: the living spirit within. At some point we will have to demonstrate what we have done with this gift. Our responsibility is to increase the gift of Spirit, not bury it. The entire purpose of giving us the gift of the living spirit within, the substance of God, is so we can multiply that substance. Just as in the parable of the seeds, the point is to increase the substance of God, the living spirit, and not let it go to waste. We are here in this world, with this body, for the purpose of making the spirit within us grow.

(42) Jesus said, "Become passers-by."

It is only the bystander, the passer-by, that dares ask, Are we the pawns, the prize, or the players? Becoming strongly involved in the ways of the world blinds us to other possibilities. Only when we step back and observe from an unattached perspective does our vision clear and we see what is happening. This is the first step in the process of spiritual growth: observation. By observing the back-and-forth exchanges between the emotions and intellectual conclusions we can see how the ego is manipulating and controlling us. We will then be in a position to recognize the traumas, programming and imprinting which have formed our personality. The recognition of the elements of the personality (ego) gives us a basic map, from which we can begin the process of inner unification and transformation.

(43) His disciples said to him, "Who are You, that You should say these things to us." Jesus said to them, "You do not realize who I am from what I say to you, but you have become like the Jews, for they either love the tree and hate its fruit, or love the fruit and hate the tree."

Truth is not something people really want. Truth defies conventional wisdom; it bruises egos, tells people that what they have learned from the world doesn't work, and brings them face-to-face with the necessity of change. We may think being in the presence of a true spiritual teacher would be a wonderful experience, but the function of the teacher is to get you to confront the issues within that keep you out of the Kingdom of Heaven. This is why the disciples respond by asking, "Who are You, that You should say these things to us?" Who does this Jesus think he is, anyway?

The true spiritual teacher may appear very superior at one moment and very vulnerable the next. When we look at spiritual teachers through the eyes of the world, we become very confused about who they really are. They are not what we expect. It helps if we remember these teachers are in the world, but not of the world. It is only when the spirit within each of us awakens that we begin to clearly see who and what these spiritual teachers really are.

Sometimes we love the tree and hate its fruit, or we love the fruit and hate the tree. What this means is that we sometimes love to feel superior to others, but hate how we have no close friends. We want our ego but don't like what we end up doing in our relationships. We often don't understand why we hurt the ones we love the most. We may rationalize it with "that's just how families are," or "this is for your own good," but dysfunctional families are the result of out-of-control egos. Substance abuse is also an ego which is out of control, saying, "I am going to do this no matter what the consequences are." The ego wants what it wants; it doesn't really care about anything else.

The spirit within us cares. This is the only real base for love we that have. But giving up the ego seems like giving up who we are, and we hate to do that. We can love the spirit within but hate to give up the ego and what it wants. We can't have it both ways. We have to choose.

(44) Jesus said, "Whoever blasphemes against the Father will be forgiven, and whoever blasphemes against the Son will be forgiven, but whoever blasphemes against the Holy Spirit will not be forgiven either on earth or in heaven."

To blaspheme is to speak of something sacred in a disrespectful way. We can speak about God or the spirit within (the Son) in a disrespectful way and it can be overcome in our spiritual growth process. The Holy Spirit can be equated with the personal experience of the presence of God. This personal experience performs all of the functions usually associated with the Holy Spirit. Through this experience come insights, revelations, guidance and even specific words that need to be said.

The presence of God is a very sensitive thing; it will not intrude where it is not welcome. Someone this author personally knows started having one of these intense experiences of the presence of God. He felt like he was losing control - that the experience was too intense. All he did was think the word "stop", and the experience instantly ended. He later expressed great regret that he had not allowed the experience to continue. Lesser versions of the experience did return to him over time and with a great amount of spiritual work, but the full intense experience of the presence of God did not return.

Our thoughts and attitudes are the things which steer our consciousness in specific directions. The effect can be profound and long-lasting. It is important to take our spiritual growth seriously. There are many side trips which the ego offers to us on our spiritual journey. Most seem harmless and can be very entertaining. But we must realize that the ego has a hidden agenda; by sidetracking our spiritual growth it remains in control of our life. We have the story of Jesus being tempted by Satan during his 40 days in the wilderness. Satan is not a person nor an evil spirit. The word is translated from Hebrew and simply means someone or something which opposes. The ego fits this description in every detail. It opposes the awakening and raising-up of the spirit within us.

The cosmic drama of God the Creator fighting against the rebellious Satan is the internal struggle between the spirit within and the ego. We are not the prize which goes to the victor of this contest; we decide the outcome. We are in control. We are not poor helpless sinners who need to be saved; we are the creators of our life experience. We create our own salvation through the process of spiritual growth. By taking control of our thoughts, feelings and actions, we take control of our life. By steering our consciousness into the presence of God and raising the level of our consciousness so the experience of that presence can be maintained, we enter the Kingdom of Heaven. If we are disrespectful to that presence, it will not come and we will not experience our salvation.

(45) Jesus said, "Grapes are not harvested from thorns, nor are figs gathered from thistles, for they do not produce fruit. A good man brings forth good from his treasure; an evil man brings forth evil things from his storehouse, which is his heart, and says evil things. For out of the abundance of the heart he brings forth evil things."

The evil things in this world stem directly from people's egos. War, starvation, poverty and the vast majority of the suffering we see is the direct result of someone's ego. The ego believes in lack. It believes that if it is to prosper it must be done at someone else's expense. In order for me to win, you have to lose. The ego rationalizes its actions as competition, telling us that competition is good for everyone. Competition means lower prices and better service; everyone wins. But competition is the base for all of the evils in the world. Let us keep in mind that war is the ultimate competition. Some of the terms for war have found their way into business. "We're going to make a killing" and "we're going to bury our competitor" are simple examples. *The Art of War* by Sun Su is required reading in a number of large corporations. Competition means someone always has to lose.

What would the world be like if we changed from competition to cooperation? My guess is that war would end first, with hunger close behind. We currently grow enough food to easily feed the world. Most disease and illness could be conquered. Poverty can be eliminated. Almost every form of suffering can be alleviated through cooperation. Cooperation could turn this world into heaven on earth. It should come as no surprise, then, that the desire for cooperation is spirit-based rather than ego-based.

(46) Jesus said, "Among those born of woman, from Adam until John the Baptist, there is no one superior to John the Baptist that his eyes should not be lowered before him. Yet I have said, whichever of you will become a child will know the Kingdom and will become superior to John."

Born of woman is born of the flesh and the inner or esoteric meaning is the ego. Of all the egos, none is superior to John the Baptist. Does this mean John had the biggest ego ever? Here superior does not mean bigger; superior means most highly developed and refined. To help understand this we must take a look at what John was saying and doing. John's focus is on religion and following the laws of God. He is going after the leaders telling them they are violating God's laws and that they must repent: change their ways and return to God. It is clear to John that adherence to the scriptural rules, the law of God, is the highest calling a person can answer. Today's ministers answer that same call.

John represents the ego. The highest level the ego can attain is to teach and follow the laws of God, the scriptural rules. As we learned in saying #4, the ego realizes that it is not the spirit. "Whichever of you will become a child will know the Kingdom" is referring to spiritual awakening and entering into the presence of God. The reference to becoming a child is referring to a state of innocence or purity of intention. This is the state attained through the work of forgiveness and results from the removal of the ego from our consciousness. Through the process of forgiveness (inner purification) the presence of God enters our lives and we come to know the Kingdom.

(47) Jesus said, "It is impossible for a man to mount two horses or to stretch two bows. And it is impossible for a servant to serve two masters; otherwise he will honor the one and insult the other. No man drinks old wine and immediately desires to drink new wine. And new wine is not put into old wineskins, lest they burst; nor is old wine put into a new wineskin, lest it spoil. An old patch is not sewn onto a new garment, because a rent would result."

Remember, this is all about consciousness. We cannot hold on to two different levels of consciousness at the same time. We cannot be spirit-based and ego-based at the same time. We have to choose. Which are we going to serve, the spirit or the ego?

The wine represents our belief system, one new and the other old. The old belief system is ego-based and the new is spirit-based. The new beliefs and consciousness cannot be put into the old belief system without bursting the old system. New wine is active and expanding; old wine is not. The new spirit-based consciousness is in the process of expanding and will tear the old system apart in the process. Nor can the ideas and practices of the ego be placed within the realm of the spirit, lest it spoil. The two systems are not compatible. The old patch and the new garment are the same analogy.

(48) Jesus said, "If two make peace with each other in this one house, they will say to the mountain, Move away and it will move away."

Once the ego and spirit come to a common goal the process of inner unification is well underway. When the ego and spirit act together, great changes can be made in the belief system. One of the exercises in Sun-do (part of the Korean system of spirituality) is, embrace tiger; release mountain. The tiger represents our fears. By embracing, or facing, our fears we come to realize that they are not real. The vast majority of our fear-based (ego-based) emotions are learned responses. And just as we learned these responses in the past, we can unlearn them now. By conquering our inner fears we release the great burden they have imposed on us for years. We feel lighter and freer. We have released the mountain which has held us down.

The mountain is the restrictive emotional base and belief system we have built up over the years. All the negative, fear-based emotions the ego uses to manipulate and control us can, and must be dismantled and removed. It is through the process of inner unification, the surrender of the ego to the spirit, making them one, which allows us to dismantle and remove the mountain.

(49) Jesus said, "Blessed are the solitary and elect, for you will find the Kingdom. For you are from it, and to it you will return."

We can view the ego-based personality as if it were a large mirror which has been dropped on a tile floor. It has shattered into many different pieces. Each piece represents a separate state of consciousness, a learned behavior which we have adopted as the result of physical or emotional trauma, programming or imprinting. Each piece has its own voice, which we received from a parent, role model, authority figure - anyone who has had an influence over us.

When a specific condition is present, we instinctively reach back into our base of experience to see how this situation was handled in the past. If we have had a parent deal with the same or very similar condition in the past, chances are we will act in the same way and do the same thing our parent has done. This is the result of imprinting. The same body language, words and tone of voice are used which have been imprinted from our childhood. Many times we think this is just the way we are, but that is not really true; it is the posture, words and tone of voice of someone else. This is a piece of the broken mirror. And this piece is activated only under certain conditions. This is because each piece has an imbedded issue, and whenever this issue comes up, this piece gets activated.

These separate issues are usually not compatible with one another. The only way for more than one conflicting issue to exist within us is to isolate each issue from the others, allowing each piece to believe it is a whole thing. In order to make this happen, a mechanism called a buffer is created. The buffer allows each conflicting piece to be experienced as the "only" piece, leaving us with the illusion of one whole being, not a fractured personality. Once we are in that personality piece, none of the other pieces seem to exist. We are consciously aware of only one piece at a time.

The ego likes to maintain the illusion that there is only one being, so it uses the buffer to isolate the consciousness of each piece from all the other pieces. The buffer is experienced as a momentary disorientation. This disorientation allows the ego to shift from one personality piece to another without it being too obvious to us. Once the situation is over, we again experience the momentary disorientation as we shift back into one of the main pieces of our personality. The disorientation occurs quickly and generally goes un-noticed. Once you know what to look for, with some practice, you will discover the buffers.

It is this fractured nature of our personality which prevents the presence of God from entering into our life experience. There is no room, no suitable place for it to be at home within us. It is up to us to make room. It is like the story of Joseph and Mary arriving in Bethlehem. There was no room at the inn, so the Christ could not be born there. When there is no room within us, the Christ Consciousness cannot be born there, either. It is up to us to unify the fractured self within, making it love-based, not fear-based, so the presence of God will have a suitable home; so the Christ child will be welcome in the inn.

Through the forgiveness process, each fractured personality piece is identified; the issue within the piece is addressed and resolved, thus dissolving the piece. The knowledge gained from resolving the issue is retained; all the rest of it can be discarded. The inner words, the attitude, the emotions and posturing involved in this issue are all stage props for the ego. They have no real value, once the issue is resolved, and thus need to be discarded.

In this way we gradually integrate the personality pieces into a real whole which is spirit-based. The separate voices are gradually eliminated, leaving only one voice: the voice of the spirit within. This one voice is referred to as being solitary. The voice of the spirit within has been raised to the level of highest importance, and thus has become the elect. It is the unified self, based on the spirit within, which finds the Kingdom. The spirit within is from God and it is the only aspect of us which can return to the presence of God.

(50) Jesus said, "If they say to you, 'Where did you come from?,' say to them, 'We came from the Light, the place where the Light came into being on its own accord and established itself and became manifest through their image.' If they say to you 'Is it you?' say 'We are its children, and we are the elect of the Living Father.' If they ask you, 'What is the sign of your Father in you?' say to them, 'It is movement and it is rest.'"

Our individual spirit comes from God. The nature of that spirit is living light. We have come from the Light (God) where the Light (note the use of upper case – referring to God) came into being of its own accord and established itself and became manifest through their image. The presence of God becomes manifest when we complete the process of inner unification. The light of spirit grows and intensifies as we imbed ourselves deeper into the Kingdom. Eventually, the presence of God is the only activating force in our lives; our actions and words become the actions and words of the Spirit working through us. Some may confuse this with thinking we are God. This is not true; we are the children of God, and as unified inner beings, the spirit within has become the solitary, and the elect of the Living Father (Spirit).

The sign of the spirit within us is first of all movement. Our spirit is the source of our individual life; without it the body does not live. Rest is the deep abiding peace which results from the process of inner unification and living in the presence of God. The combination of movement and rest is the sign of the Father in us.

(51) His disciples said to Him, "When will the repose of the dead come about, and when will the new world come?" He said to them, "What you look forward to has already come, but you do not recognize it."

This saying is one of the reasons *The Gospel of Thomas* was not selected for inclusion in the New Testament by the early Christian Church. This question is about the End Times. It assumes an outer interpretation where the coming of the new world will be a collective experience, one which happens to everybody at the same time. Jesus is explaining that it has already happened, but they do not recognize it, which renders the coming of the new world an individual experience, which must individually be entered into. "The new world" is not a physical one, but one of a new consciousness. This is the same Kingdom of Heaven Jesus has been talking about all along.

While the outer interpretation of the End Times has changed over time with the inclusion of various things which are supposed to happen, the inner experience of the Kingdom of Heaven has remained consistent. Everyone who has entered that state of consciousness has experienced the same thing; the deep abiding peace, the unconditional love which comes from God, the joy and the presence of God in their lives. Each person has become transformed by the experience and has entered into a new world, living in the presence of God.

(52) His disciples said to Him,"Twenty-four prophets spoke in Israel, and all of them spoke in You." He said to them, "You have omitted the one living in your presence and have spoken (only) of the dead."

Most of what Jesus was teaching is not new. It is the continuation of a teaching which has been around since about 1500 BCE. The prophets spoke of essentially the same thing Jesus was saying and the disciples recognize that. The sad part is that people generally will recognize the wisdom of a teacher who has been dead for several hundred years, but cannot believe the same wisdom can be found in a living person.

God is not relegated to history. God is a living experience, always in the present moment. God exists in the eternal now and each person who enters into the Kingdom of Heaven also comes into the eternal now. This is why the disciples are confused about the new world and the End Times. They think it has to be something which happens in the physical world, but it is not. This is why Jesus tells us the Kingdom of Heaven is at hand; it is a state of consciousness which exists only in the present moment. There is no past in God, there is only here and now. The same is true of prophets; they are in the here and now.

(53) His disciples said to Him, "Is circumcision beneficial or not?" He said to them, "If it were beneficial, their father would beget them circumcised from their mother. Rather the true circumcision in spirit has become completely profitable!"

The true circumcision in spirit is the cutting away of the ego, the false self. Stevan Davies[3] uses "entirely beneficial" in place of "completely profitable" above. John Dart and Ray Riegert[4] use "completely useful" in place of "completely profitable". The point is that cutting away the unnecessary part from around the spirit within is a very useful and beneficial practice. The ego, the false self, stands between us and the presence of God in our lives. If we are to enter into that consciousness the ego must be cut away and discarded.

(54) Jesus said, "Blessed are the poor, for yours is the Kingdom of Heaven."

This saying has an historical reference to it. The "poor" or the "poor in spirit" are references to the communal groups of the Essenes and similar organizations which have renounced personal property. The community provides all needed food, shelter and tools. The focus of these groups is the inner transformation and unification of the true self which leads to the experience of the Kingdom of Heaven. These groups are branches of the mystery school system and all teach the basics of spiritual-based consciousness.

(55) Jesus said, "Whoever does not hate his father and mother cannot become a disciple to Me. And whoever does not hate his brothers and sisters and take up his cross in My way will not be worthy of Me."

This concept will be visited again in saying #101. Family dynamics play a huge role in forming our ego and its personality. Sometimes we are programmed into believing the family is all important, and sometimes an abusive or neglectful family environment is replaced with a fantasy version where everything is wonderful in the mind of the person abused or neglected. Many people live in denial of what their family life actually was. Living in this kind of denial makes it much more difficult to address and resolve the inner issues necessary for spiritual growth. The person who is openly resentful toward other family members is usually much more in touch with their inner feelings. Not having to overcome the denial of what happened in the family makes the process of inner transformation easier and faster.

Each family produces some amount of trauma in the process of children growing up. Even if the parents are doing a really good job of raising their children, a trauma does not have to be real or serious, only perceived on the part of the child. The key here is not the actual trauma, but the impact it has had on the ego. It is the effect of the trauma, or perceived trauma, which must be resolved. Remember, it is not the outer conditions which separate us from God, it is the inner ones. The negative conclusions and feelings we have made and harbor regarding ourselves are the things that separate us from the presence of God. By resolving the inner issues with the intention of making room for the presence of God, the experience will come to us.

(56) Jesus said, "Whoever has come to understand the world has found a corpse, and whoever has found a corpse is superior to the world."

When you understand how the ego works and how it interacts with other egos, you will understand the world. All ego based consciousness will perish, and can be considered a corpse. Once you realize that everything associated with the ego will die, you have taken the first real step toward spiritual growth and enlightenment. You now understand there is an alternative which leads to eternal life and permanent consciousness in the presence of God. This realization places you far ahead of the vast majority of people in this world.

(57) Jesus said, "The Kingdom of the Father is like a man who has good seed. His enemy came by night and sowed weeds among the good seed. The man did not allow them to pull up the weeds; he said to them, I am afraid that you will go intending to pull up the weeds and pull up the wheat along with them. For on the day of the harvest the weeds will be plainly visible, and they will be pulled up and burned."

This is the description of inner spiritual growth. We begin with good seed, good ideas. But in our ignorance (came by night) we have adopted ideas which are not good, false ideas (weeds). When we are young we lack the experience and basic human wisdom to effectively separate the good ideas from the false ones. It is only when we mature as adult people (the day of the harvest) that we can begin to see clearly what is valuable and what is not. Just as grain is not harvested in a single day, so too does the separation of truth from falsehood take time.

The harvesting process begins with the separation of the weeds from the wheat. The weeds are thrown in a pile and burned. This, effectively, is what we do when we separate the main ideas of truth from the obvious ideas of falsehood. The false is discarded and destroyed. Next comes the separation of the chaff from the grain. This is where we take the grain of truth in each situation in our life and separate it from the outer circumstances in which it appears. We are separating what we learned from the conditions of the event.

Life is like birthdays or Christmas. We get packages with gifts hidden within. We don't know what the gift is until we open the package. Once the gift is revealed, we can discard the packaging and keep the gift. In life, we tend to hang on to the package (what happened to us) without opening it and revealing the gift inside (the lesson learned). Once we learn the lesson life has brought to us, we can discard what happened to us.

(58) Jesus said, "Blessed is the man who has suffered and found Life."

Stevan Davies[5] and John Dart with Ray Riegert[6] use the word labored in place of suffered. This is an excellent choice of words, for the inner spiritual growth process takes work, and this is not something which happens by itself. It is a consciousness which we enter into intentionally and sometimes with great effort. In the beginning the goal is awakening, but this simply marks the end of one journey and the beginning of another.

The Sufis have told us there are two journeys; the journey to God, and the journey in God. Spiritual awakening (enlightenment) is the common ground between the two journeys. As a result, spiritual growth should be considered a life-long practice. The more time and effort that is put into spiritual growth, the deeper you can move into the Kingdom of Heaven. The experiences become deeper and more profound and the understanding becomes clearer as you get deeper into the Kingdom. It's a progressive process.

The beginning goal is to find and experience the spirit within. This takes persistent effort and some dedication. But once we find the spirit within, we have found our personal source of life and begin to see how it is connected to all life and the source of all which is. This is the main turning point; finding the spirit within, the source of our life.

> **(59) Jesus said, "Take heed of the Living One while you are alive, lest you die and seek Him and be unable to see Him."**

Here the translation by Stevan Davies[7] can help clarify the saying for us.

> **(59) Jesus said: Look at the living one while you live, for if you die and then try to see him you will not be able to do so.**

The spirit within is the living one, our personal source of life, which separates from the body at the time of death. Once the body is gone, we no longer have the mechanism for producing the type of energy required to feed, awaken and empower the spirit. It is only when we have developed this 100% full conscious contact with God that we can afford to separate ourselves from the body. Until we reach that point we are wholly dependant upon the physical body for the energy necessary for our spiritual growth. This is why we choose to embed ourselves in the physical body in the first place; it provides us with the equipment and tools necessary for our spiritual growth.

We are given a specific time frame to complete our spiritual growth: a life time. The physical body wears out. It is subject to accidental damage and death; it is here for a relatively short period of time. It is critical that we focus and persist in our spiritual work once we have discovered a suitable path for our return to the presence of God. Life is very distracting and its essence slips away before we are aware of its passing. We must keep our attention on the spirit within and persist in the practice of eliminating everything which stands between us and the presence of God.

(60) They saw a Samaritan carrying a lamb on his way to Judea. He said to His disciples, "Why does that man carry the lamb around?" They said to Him, "So that he may kill and eat it." He said to them, "While it is alive, he will not eat it, but only when he has killed it and it has become a corpse." They said to Him "He cannot do otherwise." He said to them, "You too, look for a place for yourselves within the Rest, lest you become a corpse and be eaten."

The Rest is the deep abiding peace which comes from living in the presence of God. Nothing short of that will save us. In Matthew 7:13-14 (RSV) Jesus tells us, "Enter by the narrow gate, for the gate is wide and the way is easy that leads to destruction, and those who enter by it are many. For the gate is narrow and the way is hard that leads to life, and those who find it are few."

It is easy to believe, and many do. It is difficult to actually do the inner spiritual work, and few are willing to do it. Jesus tells us it is what is in our heart that is important, not what is in our mind. Our level of spiritual development is determined by our base emotional state, not by what we believe. It is only by removing the lower negative emotional states that we can elevate our base emotional state and move ourselves closer, and eventually into the Kingdom of Heaven.

(61) Jesus said, "Two will rest on a bed: the one will die, and the other will live." Salome said, "Who are you, man, that You, as though from the One, have come up on my couch and eaten from my table?" Jesus said to her, "I am He who exists from the Undivided. I was given some of the things of My Father." Salome said, "I am your disciple." Jesus said to her, "Therefore I say, if he is undivided, he will be filled with light, but if he is divided, he will be filled with darkness."

Two will rest on a bed: the one will die, and the other will live. This is the physical body and the spirit within. The physical body will die but the spirit within will live, for the spirit has eternal life as one of its qualities. The spirit is living light, the substance of God from which it was created.

Many spiritual sayings have several levels of meaning. "I am He who exists from the undivided" can refer to the spirit which exists from the substance of God. It can also refer to the consciousness which is developed from the spiritual growth process. Sayings which have several different levels of meaning are often used as a subtle test to see where the students are in their spiritual understanding. In this example, seeing that spirit is living light from the substance of God is a perception experienced earlier on in the spiritual growth process. Recognizing the nature of the emerging consciousness into an undivided state is a more advanced perception.

Jesus said, "I was given some of the things of My Father." This tells us more about how the spiritual growth process works. We begin with only an intellectual concept of God and the spirit. Through learning and practice we begin having spiritual experiences, and by this process gain more knowledge and understanding. As we become more unified we gradually gain more spiritual attributes, such as a greater depth of insight into people or, later on, the ability to heal other people. The deeper we progress into oneness and the Kingdom of Heaven, the more of these spiritual attributes we acquire.

This is the same process we use in this world as good parents. Our primary function as a parent is to prepare our children to function effectively in the world. As part of the training, we gradually give more responsibility to our children as they mature. In this process the emerging adults gradually build a base of skills which will serve them effectively in dealing with other people, building a career and raising their own family. Spiritual growth follows the same pattern. God allows more of the Spirit to flow through us and demonstrate itself in more ways as we mature spiritually.

Jesus said, "Therefore I say, if he is undivided, he will be filled with light, but if he is divided, he will be filled with darkness." This is the fractured nature of the ego-based personality which is transformed into the undivided spirit-based individuals we are meant to be. Darkness represents ignorance, and light represents knowledge and understanding. Light also represents the presence of spirit. The stronger the spirit becomes, the stronger the light within becomes. Again there are multiple levels of meaning, based on multiple levels of spiritual development. Spiritual teaching and advanced spiritual states are always about consciousness. The unification of the true self is the unification of consciousness, centered around the spirit within.

(62) Jesus said, "It is to those who are worthy of My mysteries that I give My mysteries: Do not let your left hand know what your right hand is doing."

As we have come to recognize, spiritual growth is a compounding process of learning, practice, experiences and the evolving understanding of our true spiritual nature. The spiritual mysteries are difficult for the general public to understand. It takes time and effort to learn the intellectual concepts involved in the spiritual growth process. It takes at least some dedication to do the exercises which will bring about the spiritual experiences and deeper understanding. We become worthy by persisting in trying to learn, practice and understand.

The left hand represents our ego and the right hand represents the spirit within. In the beginning of the spiritual growth process, the ego may be excited about all the new information. But once the actual work begins, the ego quickly understands that the end result of the spiritual growth process is the destruction of the ego. The ego opposes and tries to derail the process in an effort to maintain control over us. By confronting this opposition directly, we simply create more internal conflict and resistance to the spiritual growth process. The recommended process is therefore to continue doing the simple spiritual growth exercises without directly involving or confronting the ego. In the end, the tools of the ego are quietly removed and the ego must finally surrender to the spirit within.

(63) Jesus said, "There was a rich man who had much money. He said, I shall put my money to use so that I shall lack nothing. Such were his intentions, but that same night he died. Let him who has ears hear."

We are given a limited amount of time in this world to accomplish our spiritual growth. We do not know if today is our last day on earth or not. The temptation is to do our spiritual growth work when we can fit it into our schedule. There is the story of the university professor who puts on a demonstration for each freshman class. He takes several large rocks and puts them into a large glass container. He then asks the class if the container is full. It is obvious that no more rocks can be added so the class answers "Yes, the container is full." The professor then takes small rocks and adds them to the container, filling up the spaces between the large rocks. Again he asks the question "Is the container full?" And again the class answers "Yes." The professor now pours sand into the container, filling up the smaller spaces, and again asks if the container is full. Again the class answers "Yes." The professor then adds water to the container and again asks if the container is full. Now the class is sure of its answer: "Yes, now it is full." The professor then slowly adds some salt to the container which dissolves into the water. The professor now asks, "What have we learned from the experiment?" The class offers many explanations but misses the point, so the professor explains, "If you don't put the large rocks in first, you'll never get them in at all. If you don't do the things which are the most important first, you'll never get them done."

The point of the story is that spiritual growth is the one thing which will move us out of the suffering and death the world offers and into the peace, love, joy and eternal life which God offers. If we don't do our spiritual growth first, it won't get done.

(64) Jesus said, "A man received visitors. And when he had prepared dinner, he sent his servant to invite the guests. He went to the first one and said to him, 'My master invites you.' He said 'I have claims against some merchants. They are coming to me this evening. I must go and give them my orders. I ask to be excused from the dinner.' He went to another and said to him, 'My master has invited you.' He said to him, 'I have just bought a house and am required for the day. I shall not have any spare time.' He went to another and said, 'My master invites you.' He said to him, 'My friend is going to get married, and I am to prepare the banquet. I shall not be able to come. I ask to be excused from the dinner.' He went to another and said to him, 'My master invites you.' He said to him, 'I have just bought a farm, and am on my way to collect the rent. I shall not be able to come. I ask to be excused.' The servant returned and said to his master, 'Those whom you have

invited to the dinner have asked to be excused.' The master said to his servant, 'Go outside to the streets and bring back those whom you happen to meet, so that they may dine. Traders and merchants will not enter the places of My Father.'"

In the time of Jesus the mystery school system had become an organization which catered to the wealthy and powerful. The system was designed to protect and conceal the spiritual truth from lower class people. The problem Jesus encountered was that the wealthy and powerful were not interested in actually doing the work of spiritual growth – in this example, attending the dinner. The wealthy and powerful are convinced their lives are working well for them and are not in need of change. The excuses offered above demonstrate the dedication to the things of the world, rather than the things of God represented by the dinner or banquet.

This is Jesus' explanation of why he began teaching ordinary people about the Kingdom of Heaven. The tax collectors, prostitutes and other lower class people to whom Jesus is accused of revealing the forbidden spiritual knowledge to already know their lives are not working, and they are open to change. These are the people who are willing to dedicate themselves to a true spiritual path and do whatever is required to change their lives. These people are represented by those "whom you happen to meet" in the streets. The Kingdom of Heaven is open to anyone who will do the work required to enter into that level of consciousness.

(65) He said, "There was a good man who owned a vineyard. He leased it to tenant farmers so that they might work it and he might collect the produce from them. He sent his servant so that the tenants might give him the produce of the vineyard. They seized his servant and beat him, all but killing him. The servant went back and told his master. The master said, 'Perhaps they did not recognize him.' He sent another servant. They beat him as well. Then the owner sent his son and said, 'Perhaps they will show respect to my son.' Because the tenants knew that it was he who was the heir to the vineyard, they seized him and killed him. Let him who has ears hear."

The concept of a Son of God being seized and killed was not a new idea in the time of Jesus. Even ordinary people were familiar with several Sons of God from the past who were seized and killed. In the Middle East, people were familiar with Osiris from Egypt, Mithra from Persia, and Adad from Assyria. From a little farther away we have Chrishna of Hindustan and Buddha of India. These were the legends with which they grew up. So Jesus is using their familiarity with these teachings to demonstrate the inner nature of the ego against the spirit within.

The ego is essentially given the job of being a servant, of ordering and coordinating our life. The spirit is intended to be the recipient, or beneficiary, of the ego's work. But the ego has aspirations of its own. From our early years we begin to identify with the ego as us. What the ego wants, we want. It all becomes very simple and straightforward. The arrival of the spirit into our awareness is disturbing. Initial ideas about the presence of the spirit within and the Kingdom of Heaven are usually beaten down by the ego and dismissed. This is represented by the servants of the master being beaten by the tenants. When the spirit within (the son) makes its appearance, the ego tries to kill it. The ego generally wants nothing to do with the emerging spirit within and wants it to disappear by any means necessary.

This is why many people will insist that God is someone or something which is "out there" but cannot appear within. "Out there" is safe. "Within" is dangerous; it challenges the power and authority of the ego and its fractured personality. The presence of the spirit within and its ability to bring about the Kingdom of Heaven, true salvation and eternal life is the single most devastating challenge the ego ever faces. Everything is at risk: our belief in God, salvation, family, career, money, power, control, social position and everything else attached to life as we know it. Everything we thought we were or could be is challenged by the presence of the spirit within. If the spirit within is real, the mountain which has become our life is about to be obliterated.

Just as the tenants falsely perceive the produce from the vineyard as theirs, the ego falsely perceives the benefits of life as its own. Life is the birthright of the spirit, not the ego. The body is meant to serve the spirit within, not the ego. Our lives are constructed so that we may ultimately learn that what we see, touch and feel in life is illusion, and what we can't see and touch is real. A complete reversal in perceptions is required before we discover who and what we really are. We must unlearn the ways of the world and learn the ways of God. In doing so, we transform not only our own life, but also parts of the lives of those we encounter on our journey back to, and into, God. Indeed, this transformation is the sole purpose for life as we know it.

(66) Jesus said, "Show me the stone that the builders have rejected. That one is the cornerstone."

Cornerstones are important; they mark changes in direction, they are anchor points, places of strength firmly set on the foundation. The ego, in its desire to build its own empire, sees itself as the foundation. This is why the body is manipulated into producing the lower, negative emotions which create the energy needed to feed the ego. When the personality is fractured into separate issues and the illusion of wholeness is sustained through the use of buffers, the reality of the spirit within must be rejected. The ego ends up building a house of cards, a cardboard castle, rather than something which endures.

As we begin the process of inner unification, we select the spirit within as the cornerstone. Only the spirit within is firmly set in the foundation of God, for it is of God and not of this world. By using the spirit within as the anchor point and the means of changing direction in our life, we can set in motion the inner transformation of consciousness which leads us into the Kingdom of Heaven and eternal life. The ego will reject the spirit within, but that spirit is the cornerstone of living in the presence of God.

(67) Jesus said, "Whoever knows the All, but fails to know himself, misses everything."

Once in a while people who are not following a spiritual path will have a deep spiritual experience. What is meant to be a life changing experience becomes a strange thing that happened to them. They have experienced the presence of God, but it is so out of context with the rest of their lives that they miss the connection with the spiritual part of themselves. God and this presence and love they experienced are still outside, separate from who and what they consider themselves to be. They have come to know the “All” by having this intense spiritual experience, but having missed the connection to their own inner spiritual self, they are clueless about the ramifications of spiritual growth, true salvation and eternal life.

This is one of the reasons Jesus taught as many people as would listen to him. People have spiritual experiences. If they don’t know how these experiences relate to the spirit within, they miss the greatest opportunity of their entire lives. This is another level of understanding for saying #64 above. By living with their focus in the world, they spend their time with small, relatively unimportant things while they miss the Kingdom of Heaven. This is why an understanding of our inner spiritual nature is so important. When a deep spiritual experience comes (the invitation to dine with the Master) we need to understand the implications of what is happening to us. We are being invited into the presence of God and are being given the opportunity to enter into eternal life. If we don’t understand that connection, we miss everything.

(68) Jesus said, “Blessed are you when you are hated and persecuted. Wherever you have been persecuted they will find no place.”

This saying and the one which follows are very similar and revolve around the same issue, so we will address them together.

(69) Jesus said, “`Blessed are they who have been persecuted within themselves, it is they who have come to know the Father in Truth. Blessed are the hungry, for the belly of him who desires will be filled.”

There is no doubt practitioners of religion have been persecuted. Anything outside of the mainstream of society is subject to various types of persecution, even if it is for the improvement and benefit of that society. The esoteric teaching of Jesus deals specifically with inner issues and processes. So the reference to persecution, which saying #69 makes clear, has to do with a form of inner attack or inner persecution. The active or proactive form of self unification based on the spirit within does in fact persecute the ego. It is this inner attack and persecution, which in time dismantles the ego, that is responsible for the awakening, raising up and empowerment of the spirit which places us in the Kingdom of Heaven.

Once we realize it is the ego which stands between us and the presence of God, we are faced with the choice of remaining with the ego and living our life separated from God or persecuting and dismantling the ego and entering into life within the presence of God. This is the simple essence of the choice we have before us. We serve the ego or we serve God.

(70) Jesus said, "That which you have within you will save you if you bring it forth from yourselves. That which you do not have within you will kill you, if you do not have it inside you."

Here the translation by Stevan Davies will help us clarify the saying.

(70) Jesus said, "When you give rise to that which is within you, what you have will save you. If you do not give rise to it, what you do not have will destroy you."

Awakening, raising and empowering the spirit within is the only way to break the cycle of life and death. By giving rise to the spirit within, we can change our center of consciousness from the ego to the spirit. The spirit-centered consciousness is what saves us. Salvation is spirit centered consciousness. If we do not raise the spirit within, we have no choice but to have our consciousness fade into nothingness when the ego no longer has the body to feed and support it. Everything we have built upon the foundation of the ego will pass away; nothing will remain.

(71) Jesus said, "I shall destroy this house, and no one will be able to rebuild it."

This is a primary goal of spiritual growth: to destroy the house of the ego so that it cannot be rebuilt. As long as the ego remains it stands as a barrier to the Kingdom of Heaven. We cannot pass through into that 100% full conscious contact with God until the ego has been destroyed.

(72) A man said to Him, "Tell my brother to divide my father's possessions with me." He said to him, "Oh man, who has made Me a divider?" He turned to His disciples and said to them, "I am not a divider, am I?"

Here Jesus is having a little fun. Everything Jesus taught was for the unification of the self. In his role as a Rabbi, Jesus would be approached to help settle family disputes. Yet Jesus does not really see himself as a Rabbi but as a true spiritual teacher, one focused on inner unification of the self. For only through inner unification can we become solitary and worthy of entering into the full presence of God.

(73) Jesus said, "The harvest is great but the laborers are few. Beseech the Lord, therefore, to send out laborers to the harvest."

There are so many good people in the world who would really like to have the spiritual experiences and enter into the Kingdom of Heaven. But because of the outer expression of religion telling people all they have to do is believe, very few are willing to do the work required to actually have the experiences they seek. This is not a new condition; it has always been this way. There has always been the outer expression and the inner expression of religion. This conflict has been there from the beginning. It really doesn't matter what the religion is, for each exists in both forms. We as individuals must choose between believing and experiencing. Jesus is asking for more people who will work on their spiritual growth and not just believe.

(74) He said, "Oh Lord there are many around the well, but there is nothing in the cistern."

A large majority of the people involved in religion find it easier to believe. They flock around the various religious centers but find only other believers. They do not enter into the experience of the presence of God on a continuous basis. Many go to their churches, mosques, synagogues and temples to find God and enter into His presence. Yet all they are taught in these houses of God is to believe. God is not experienced there. Our passage to God and the Kingdom of Heaven is through the spirit within, not through an external structure or system of belief.

(75) Jesus said, "Many are standing at the door, but it is the solitary that will enter the bridal chamber."

It doesn't matter how much you believe or how much you want to enter the Kingdom of Heaven. It is only those who have gone through the process of inner unification of the self who will enter into this union of consciousness with God. Nothing of the ego may remain, no fractured pieces, no issues, no regrets or guilty feelings, anger, resentment or bitterness. Only the solitary - the unified self, centered on the spirit within, can enter completely into the full presence of God.

(76) Jesus said, "The Kingdom of the Father is like a merchant who had a consignment of goods and who discovered a pearl. That merchant was shrewd. He sold the goods and bought the pearl alone for himself. You too, seek His unfailing and enduring treasure where no moth comes near to devour and no worm destroys."

The parable of the pearl is like the parable of the fisherman. The goods of the merchant are the ideas and concepts which comprise the belief system. The merchant discovers a pearl, an idea which is much more important and valuable than the other ideas and concepts. So the merchant sells all the goods and buys the pearl. This means all the other ideas and beliefs are disposed of and the one idea is kept for himself.

Jesus tells us to seek His unfailing and enduring treasure which cannot be destroyed. That treasure is the awakened and empowered spirit within, and the eternal life which is gained by attaching our consciousness to the spirit rather than to the ego, which will fade away into nothingness. This practice of awakening the spirit within, raising and empowering that spirit and attaching our consciousness to the spirit within is the single most important idea Jesus offers. Every treasure the world has to offer can and will be taken away from you. Death will separate you from it all. Only the eternal life Jesus offers will remain.

(77) Jesus said, "It is I who am the Light which is above them all. It is I who am the All. From me did the All come forth, and unto Me did the All attain. Split a piece of wood, and I am there. Lift up a stone and you will find Me there."

There are two ways ideas come forth from a true spiritual teacher like Jesus. One is the explanations which often take the form of stories and parables. The other is the direct expression of the Spirit of God as it speaks through the teacher. This is one of those times when the Spirit of God speaks directly through Jesus. God is the Light which is above all other lights. God is both the creator and the creation. Everything which exists does so through the thought, energy and substance of God. Nothing exists that is not of God substance. The universe came forth from God, and as God substance (spirit) all is capable of returning to and attaining union with God.

In saying #19 Jesus said, "If you become My disciples and listen to My words, these stones will minister to you." This is because everything is constructed with the substance of God. It is in and of everything. "Split a piece of wood, and I am there." The substance of God is there in the wood. "Lift up a stone and you will find Me there." God is there within the stone, around the stone, and in the space where the stone was. God is everywhere, in and of everything. There is no place in the entire universe where God is not. But it is like radio waves or television signals. We can't see or hear them unless we can "tune in" to them. Without our awareness of them they simply appear not to exist, and yet the world is full of them.

God functions in a similar manner. God appears not to be there until we learn to "tune in" to the level of consciousness where we can experience the presence of God. Our failure to tune in is not proof God does not exist. If you have a television set and never turn it on, it does not mean there are no television programs. Turning the television set on will prove these programs exist. You can experience a wide variety of programs once the set is turned on. The same holds true with God. Once we awaken and turn on the spirit within, we will experience the presence of God. That experience is the proof of God's existence. Just as we might find an interesting channel on the television and tell a friend about the program and its content and how to get the station, so too do spiritual teachers tell others about God, the content of the experience, and the means of tuning in to that level of consciousness. The entire teaching of Jesus centers on the concepts and practices of tuning in to God. It's all there, once we learn what the teaching really means.

(78) Jesus said, "Why have you come out into the desert? To see a reed shaken by the wind? And to see a man clothed in soft raiment like your kings and your great men? Upon them are the fine garments, and they are unable to discern the truth."

The ego perceives things within the context of the world. If spiritual power exceeds earthly power, the ego expects to see greater earthly success in spiritual people. What the ego misses is the subject of focus. Earthly success comes from focusing on earthly things. Spiritual success comes from focusing on spiritual things. The focus on earthly things precludes the change in consciousness which is required to enter into the presence of God and God's truth. This is why Jesus said, "Upon them are the fine garments, and they are unable to discern the truth." By focusing on spiritual things in our search for the truth, we preclude great success in the world. It is rare for a spirit-based person to become even moderately wealthy, and even then they generally don't care about the money.

The search for truth is the search for something extraordinary. This is why Jesus asks, "Why have you come out into the desert? To see a reed shaken by the wind?" They have come to see something extraordinary, but the ego expects this to be something within the context of the world, and the ego is usually disappointed by what it sees. What it misses is the extraordinary experience which is taking place within the person. We are curious and intrigued by the person living within the presence of God. We want to know what it is like and what changes has this experience made in their lives. In essence, we want to know what it would be like for us to have this experience: to live in the presence of God. We imagine it to be a life-changing experience, and it is. But the change is not what we expect. The change is all internal, which means our outer life conditions often change very little. This expression sums it up well: "Before enlightenment you chop wood and carry water. After enlightenment you chop wood and carry water."

The change we are looking for is the inner transformation of consciousness, rather than worldly success. This is why Jesus commented that the wealthy and powerful of this world "have their reward." They have focused on the things of the world, and their success is their reward. By focusing on the inner spiritual being and the inner practice of self-unification, we enter into the Kingdom of Heaven and begin living our life in the presence of God. The reward for doing so is not worldly success but eternal life.

(79) A woman from the crowd said to him, "Blessed is the womb which bore You and the breasts which nourished You." He said to her, "Blessed are those who have heard the Word of the Father and have truly kept it. For there will come days when you will say, 'Blessed are the wombs which have not conceived and the breasts which have not given milk."

The world is an uncertain place and fate is fickle. What the world favors and builds at one time it attacks and destroys at another. Only the unconditional love which comes from God is stable and secure. Only the consciousness firmly centered on the spirit within and the unified inner self survives the world and enters into eternal life. "Blessed are those who have heard the Word of the Father and have truly kept it" refers to those who have ears to hear: those who have developed the understanding that every spiritual principle and saying deals with our inner thoughts and feelings. It is always about consciousness and the inner processes which lead to oneness with God and all of creation.

We become blessed not by beseeching God for favor or by proclaiming the Kingdom, but by entering into the consciousness of oneness. Seeking favor and invoking proclamations are ways of the world and as such are the tools and workings of the ego. None of these things will produce the Kingdom of Heaven. Only changing our inner state of consciousness and unifying the fractured inner self will get us into the Kingdom. Only by "hearing" and understanding the inner spiritual process, the Word of the Father, can we become blessed, and then only with a great deal of work. Spiritual growth is not luck or fate; it is the result of unlearning the ways of the world, learning the ways of God and the Spirit, and keeping those ways.

(80) Jesus said, "He who has recognized the world has found the body, but he who has found the body is superior to the world."

He who has found the body has found the ego. Recognizing that the ego is separate from the spirit is the beginning. Learning that the ego is temporary and the spirit is eternal makes you superior to the world. But this knowledge is essentially useless unless it is followed up by the inner work of spiritual growth. What we do makes the difference, not what we believe.

(81) Jesus said, "Let him who has grown rich be king, and let him who possesses power renounce it."

The ego uses wealth to acquire power, and power to acquire control. The ego sees everything and everyone as needing to be controlled, except itself. And yet, as we are learning, the #1 thing over which we can gain control is our own ego, for it stands between us and the presence of God. If we have power over others, the best application of that power is to encourage each individual to grow and become the best he can be. This means that we will ultimately lose control over others, which is why this application is practiced so rarely.

The real issue is not power itself, but the control over others it comes to represent. The desire to control others is what must be renounced. Power, like wealth, is a tool. The problem lies not in the tool, but in its application. Power and wealth can be used to implement a great deal of good in the world, but its most common use is to increase the pain and suffering of humanity. This is accomplished through the aggrandizement of one or more human egos at the expense of other people's lives.

What we do with power is strictly dependant on what is in our hearts. A good person brings forth good from his warehouse, and an evil person brings forth evil ("warehouse" signifying the heart). The feelings within us are the source of our actions. Rarely does logic dictate our actions. As long as we function from a fractured inner nature we find the unresolved issues within us dictating our actions and our lives. This is the source of evil in the actions of people in this world: the unresolved inner issues within each person. By going through a process of inner unification based on the spirit within, we resolve all of these inner issues. When we do this, the need to control others is resolved as well. We can then view wealth and power as means of implementing the growth and individuality of others, rather than as a means of control.

In his book, *The Gospel of Thomas,* Stevan Davies[8] highlights another level of understanding for this saying by relating it to saying #3. If self-knowledge leads to the realization of the spirit within, this can be expressed as a type of wealth, for its opposite, lack of self-knowledge is expressed as poverty. Ideally, those who have spiritual understanding should be the ones to rule. True spiritual understanding draws one to service, and should be the guiding quality of those who rule over others. Unfortunately, the most spiritual people do not seek public office or positions of power over others.

(82) Jesus said, "Whoever is near Me is near the fire, and he who is far from Me is far from the Kingdom."

Jesus has found the means of awakening, raising and empowering the spirit within. This is the fire, the living light of spirit, and the brighter it shines the stronger the spirit within has become. Whoever is closely following in the footsteps of Jesus, doing what he did to awaken the spirit within, is near the fire of the living light of spirit. This leads to a change of consciousness which brings us into the presence of God: into the Kingdom. Whoever is not following this inner process of unification and transformation is far from the experience of the presence of God and the Kingdom of Heaven.

(83) Jesus said, "The images are revealed to man, but the light in them remains concealed in the image of the Light of the Father. He will become manifest, but His image will remain concealed by His Light."

Our physical eyes are constructed to see the things in the world. We see the physical bodies of other people and we see our own body. What we do not see so clearly is the living light within each and every living thing. A few people can see these living lights easily, and most people can train themselves to see at least something of the light which is there. The outer manifestation of the living light within is the aura which is three dimensional, extending all around the physical body. The central driving force behind the aura is the living light of spirit within. The color of the aura is dependant on the state of the emotions and the consciousness of the individual.

As we become unified within, the variations in the light emanating from us tends to unify as well. When we move our consciousness from being ego-based to being spirit-based and enter into the presence of God, our aura turns golden in color. The stronger the spirit within becomes, the stronger the aura becomes. As God is revealed to us through the spiritual experiences we encounter, the image of the living light becomes clearer to us. Spiritual encounters with God also tend to reveal the image of God as a living light. This light is experienced as being extremely bright, but does not hurt the eyes such as bright sunlight would. Some people believe there is some kind of a being at the center of the light we perceive as God. Whatever the case may be, the true image of God is concealed within the light.

(84) Jesus said, "When you see your likeness, you rejoice. But when you see your images which came into being before you, and which neither die nor become manifest, how much will you have to bear!"

Our encounters with God change how we perceive ourself, others, and the world in which we live. We begin with the recognition of physical bodies, seeing everyone as separate beings competing for the things we need and want. On our spiritual journey within, we begin first to understand intellectually that we are actually living light, not just the physical body we see. This understanding expands to actual experiences of seeing the living light, first in others, and then in ourselves. Our encounters with God also teach us to see the living light in all things. We come to see and understand that we live in a fully connected and integrated universe.

Once the image of separation has been broken and the oneness of God and the universe has become manifest to us, the contrast shatters the old belief system. We find that the world in which we live has somehow radically changed; nothing is as it was before. Some people, when faced with this new perception, reject it and return to the perception of the world. The main reason for this refusal to accept the new perception is a lack of knowledge about inner spiritual principles and the process of inner transformation. This is one of the reasons *The Gospel of Thomas* is such an important document and why it is so important to explain the inner meanings of these sayings to as many people as possible. The more people understand about the inner workings of spirit, the more likely they are to accept the new perceptions and proceed with the process of inner unification and transformation which leads to the Kingdom of Heaven (living in the presence of God).

(85) Jesus said, "Adam came into being from a great power and a great wealth, but he did not become worthy of you. For had he been worthy, he would not have experienced death."

The mystery school system was originally created to bring the true spiritual knowledge to people. Those who were serious about their spiritual growth and disciplined enough (disciples) to practice the process of inner transformation were deemed "worthy." Over the years "worthy" changed from meaning serious students of spiritual growth to the wealthy and socially elite, all others being considered "unclean." Jesus is returning the use of the term "worthy" to its original meaning: one who is serious and dedicated to the inner spiritual practice.

(86) Jesus said, "Foxes have their holes and the birds have their nests. But the Son of Man has no place to lay his head and rest."

Foxes and birds are creatures of the world, and as such have a place in the world to rest. The Son of Man is a term referring to the spirit within each individual person. Most translations use the lower case, which as discussed before, refers to the un-awakened spirit within each individual person. The spirit within is *in* this world but it is not *of* this world, so there is no place in the world for it to rest or to be at peace. The only place for the spirit to truly rest is in the Kingdom of Heaven.

The un-awakened spirit is often referred to as sleeping, or asleep. Just as we dream, and stir occasionally when we sleep, so too does the spirit within have a certain level of activity associated with it. The restless spirit is the source of many people's drive for "finding themselves" in the world. The ego drives us to accomplish things in the world, but it is the restless spirit that seeks meaning in the things of the world, and not finding what it seeks, wanders from one thing to another. The restless spirit is seeking God and the presence of God in its life. It is no wonder it cannot find God in the world, for we must find God within ourselves before we will recognize God's presence in the world. The restless spirit is trying to awaken and is the driving force in saying #2 (Let the one seek[ing] not stop [seeking until] he finds.)

(87) Jesus said, "Wretched is the body that is dependant upon a body, and wretched is a soul that is dependant on these two."

The ego is the inner expression of the body. The world teaches our ego to manipulate others into fulfilling our inner needs. Those inner needs are: protecting our self, caring for our self, valuing our self, respecting our self and loving our self. This makes our emotional state dependant on others. Another person has neither the time nor the inclination to devote himself to making us happy. Even if he tries, he cannot succeed. Happiness is the result of entering into the love and joy which emanates from God and flows through us into the world. Another person cannot make us happy, nor can he fulfill the inner needs we each experience.

When we depend on another to fulfill our inner needs, we open ourselves to the many disappointments and emotional injuries we all suffer in life. The other day I saw a young girl walking down the street wearing a shirt with "I HAVE ISSUES" printed on it. My thought was "no kidding, welcome to planet earth." We all have issues. The part which makes us wretched is that our issues and emotional injuries take the place of the presence of God in our lives. When our life is filled with issues and we are dependant on another person to fulfill our inner needs, there is no room left for the presence of God. Unless we fulfill our own inner needs, our soul or spirit is barred from experiencing the full and complete presence of God.

We are responsible for fulfilling our own inner needs, resolving our emotional issues, and creating a suitable home within for the presence of God to enter. Each issue which is resolved provides space for some of the presence of God. As our work on unification of the self continues, we experience more and more of the presence of God in our lives. As the process of transformation becomes complete we find ourselves living completely within the presence of God, filled with peace, love and joy. We will have become one with God and one with all of creation.

> **(88) Jesus said, "The angels and the prophets will come to you and give you those things that you already have. And you too, give them what is in your hand, and say to yourselves, 'When will they come and take what is theirs?'"**

Here, the Stevan Davies translation can help us.

> **(88) Jesus said: The messengers are coming to you with the prophets, and they will give you what is properly yours. You then should give them what you have. Say to yourselves: "When will they come and take what is theirs?"**

The Father loves the Son, and everything the Father has is given to the Son. This is our inheritance. Spirit (God) creates the spirit within and as the spirit within matures, power and authority are gradually given to it. We do the same thing in the world. As our children mature we give them more power and authority over their own activities. This is part of the maturing process. We learn that authority and responsibility are two sides of the same coin; they must work together. We only create problems when we try to separate authority and responsibility.

Just as we don't toss the keys to the family car to a five year old and tell him to have fun, so too is spiritual power not given to those who are not spiritually mature. The consequences are too serious. As we grow spiritually we receive knowledge and insights as a result of our spiritual experiences. These are things which are ours as part of our inheritance, but we have not taken possession of them due to our lack of spiritual maturity. As knowledge matures into wisdom, we gradually gain the power and authority associated with the knowledge we have come to understand. These are the things we may perceive as coming from the angels and prophets.

In exchange we must give them (release) the limitations we have adopted over the years. It is like the story of Jonathan Livingston Seagull[9] where he finally comes to the realization, "Why, that's true! I *am* a perfect, unlimited gull!" We come to the realization of who and what we really are only as we give up the limitations we have imposed on our own consciousness.

When will they come and take what is theirs? When we have been given so much we wonder what we will have to give in return. What will God require of us in exchange for what we have gained? A true spiritual path will cost you everything and nothing. It will require that you give up all of your fear, anger, hatred, jealousy, envy, resentment, bitterness and pride. You will have to give up all of your limiting concepts, ideas, beliefs, feelings and thoughts of worthlessness and shame. Everything which stands between you and your full and complete conscious contact with God must go. You will give up the person you thought you were, only to have it replaced with the divine being you really are. You will find that everything you give up has no value anyway, and you are simply releasing that which has held you down for so long.

The secret is, what the angels and prophets receive, and what is theirs, is your friendship, your brotherhood or sisterhood. The bond of shared consciousness is part of the Love which emanates from God; it is unconditional and unlimited. What God requires of us is our loving service to the children of God in this world. In providing that service, we are blessed, not by receiving God's love, but by its flow as it passes through us. There is no greater love; there is no greater experience.

(89) Jesus said, "Why do you wash the outside of the cup? Do you not understand that he who made the inside is the same one who made the outside?"

While the Jewish people were unusual in their practice of washing themselves and their pots, pans and dishes, we have to keep in mind that outer examples are used to illuminate inner processes. Spiritual growth highlights the conflict between the ego and the spirit within. The ego is a manifestation of the body and the spirit is a manifestation of God. But we cannot forget that the body is also a creation of God. He who made the inside (the spirit within) is the same one who made the outside (the physical body). The main difference is in their duration. The spirit within is designed to last forever, while the physical body is temporary. The physical body, then, is a means to an end, not an end in itself.

The physical body is a temporary source of energy for us to use for our spiritual growth. Once we have established our 100% full conscious contact with God, we can tap directly into God, which is the highest source of energy for our spirit. Until then, we are limited in accessing the energy of God by our consciousness. We live in the presence of God like a fish lives in the water. Our spirit is sustained by this presence at whatever level it functions. We can gain energy and spiritual strength slowly by the changing of our consciousness alone, but God has provided a way for us to accelerate our growth process by using the physical body to produce the specific type of energy the spirit within needs to grow rapidly. As such, we can experience the evolution of our spirit into a fully awakened and empowered being within one lifetime, rather than over many lifetimes.

This is the underlying secret of the mystery school system: God has given us a way to accelerate our spiritual growth and complete the entire process in one lifetime, if we will learn to use the physical body properly. The body is an energy transformation machine, and we tell the body what form of energy to produce by the emotions we experience. The lower (negative) emotions tell the body to produce the energy needed by the ego, and the higher emotions of love and compassion tell the body to produce the energy needed by the spirit within. The results we experience are determined not by the emotions of a passing moment, but by which emotions dominate our lives the vast majority of the time.

Just as the washing of the cup illustrates, there is a cleansing process for both the mind and the emotions. Both our thoughts and feelings must be transformed, if we are to be transformed spiritually. This is what the spiritual exercises are designed to accomplish. This is why Jesus repeatedly talked about forgiveness. When we forgive both mentally and emotionally, we free ourselves from the past. We are then free to choose our own emotions in the present rather than being trapped into experiencing the emotions of the past. Our past sins (the negative thoughts and feelings in the past) can be washed away (transformed into love and compassion) through salvation (the awakening and empowerment of the spirit within).

(90) Jesus said, "Come unto Me, for My yoke is easy and My Lordship is mild, and you will find rest for yourselves."

Sometimes religious practices can be taken to extremes. Some organizations require people to prove themselves by enduring a number of physical and emotional hardships. None of these things are actually required for spiritual growth. The only thing they do is establish dominance over the person going through the process. A true spiritual path is about inner transformation. There are specific exercises which help us release ourself from the control of the ego, but these are far from harsh. Specific meditation-type practices done for 15 to 20 minutes, two to three times a day are quite sufficient. Effort is also required in becoming more aware and observant of our thoughts and feelings during the day. This is easy and mild, compared with many religious practices.

Spiritual growth is the result of focused techniques designed to dismantle the ego and the emotional tools it uses to control us. The work is not hard but it does require persistence. The process can be likened to emptying a swimming pool one cup at a time. We are removing only a small amount at any given time, but the accumulated effect produces the end result we need. Step by step we enter into the presence of God and we gradually come into the deep abiding peace which is the rest of which Jesus speaks. Spiritual growth is not about obedience or sacrifice, but rather inner transformation and unification of the self.

(91) They said to Him, "Tell us who You are that we may believe in You." He said to them, "You read the face of the sky and of the earth, but you have not recognized the One who is before you, and you do not know how to read this moment."

Religion is about believing; spirituality is about becoming. These are two entirely different processes and they produce two entirely different results and experiences. Believing results in placing your trust and faith in something, or someone, outside of yourself. Becoming results in an inner transformation and brings you into direct conscious contact with God.

Many people want to understand the spiritual sayings and principles. They perceive this in the same way they were taught in school: When you learn to repeat back specific facts, you have learned what is being taught. But spiritual growth is more like real life: We learn through our experiences, by doing the things which need to be done first, and then deriving the understanding from our experiences. This book is designed to help you get an intellectual understanding of what spiritual growth is about. But your growth will not take place without doing the specific exercises. The exercises are designed to create an inner transformation which brings about specific spiritual experiences. These spiritual experiences will bring you the actual and real understanding of God and your true spiritual nature. Believing is not required. When we do the exercises, have the spiritual experiences, and enter into the presence of God, we gain direct knowledge of God (*gnosis*). This is the whole point of the teachings of Jesus.

The problem the disciples are having is that the ego cannot see the spirit within someone else. They don't know whether to believe Jesus or not. This is the problem everyone faces with a true spiritual teacher: that of not knowing if he is for real or not. This is why Jesus uses parables about trees bearing fruit; you come to know people by what they actually do in real life. Is this teacher really trying to teach, or is it about money or domination? A true spiritual teacher teaches out of a desire to be of service to others, not to have others serve him.

(92) Jesus said, "Seek and you shall find. Yet, what you asked Me about in former times and which I did not tell you then, now I wish to tell, but you do not inquire after it."

Spiritual growth is a process, and the truth we arrive at early in our journey may be suitable for us then, but we may have outgrown that meaning later on. The spiritual journey is an ongoing process of re-evaluating past information and beliefs. Spiritual growth is a constant process of refining our knowledge and understanding of God. Many of the conclusions we come to make sense at the time, but with an expanding consciousness will need to be revised. New information takes the place of the old just as our new consciousness takes the place of the older, lower level of consciousness. The key is not to get stuck. When we read a book and something really speaks to us, we don't stop reading the rest of the book. A spiritual journey is the same way. Just because you find something really meaningful to you, don't get stuck on it; keep growing and moving forward.

(93) Jesus said, "Do not give what is holy to the dogs, lest they throw them on the dung heap. Do not cast pearls to swine, lest they grind it to bits."

Many people will not accept the inner teaching. This is OK. The word esoteric also means "meant for the few". What it really comes down to is that only a few will accept the inner teaching and follow it. So the different meanings of esoteric (inner and meant for the few) are inter-related by function. This is not a debate. Either a person will see the value of the inner path (eyes to see) or they won't. Either the explanations make sense (ears to hear) or they don't. It's really that simple.

This teaching is not spread by force of belief or logical argument. It spreads by the gentle stirring and awakening of the spirit within. We determine whether a person is open to the process by introducing a small amount of new information to him.

If the reaction is positive and he seems open to more, we share a little more. Learning is a prolonged step-by-step process. You didn't go from kindergarten to a senior in high school in a week. Learning and the growth associated with it take time. If a person is not open to the inner path, don't continue to share the inner information with him. Share only where the information is valued and accepted.

(94) Jesus said, "He who seeks will find, and (he who knocks) will be let in."

The most important aspect of spiritual growth is persistence. The exercises are not complicated; anyone can do them. Sometimes the emotional issues we have to work through are painful, and it takes a certain amount of courage to face the pain inside of us. Like saying #2, we need to continue to seek until we find. We need to continue on with the exercises until we establish our 100% full conscious contact with God. The bottom line is this: If you persist, you will succeed.

(95) Jesus said, "If you have money do not lend it at interest, but give to one from whom you will not get it back."

The spiritual-based person sees the importance of being of service to others rather than having others of service to him. Money is a tool which helps us survive in the world. It buys food, clothing and shelter. Money makes life easier and more comfortable. These are all important things. But a large amount of money, rather than allowing us to be of greater service to others, often tends to isolate us from other people. Wealth often engenders a sense of superiority in people, which isolates them even more. Truly being of service to others reconnects us with others and brings us closer to God in the process. It is not necessary, nor is it advisable, to give all of our money away. But what you can comfortably do without, use in service to others. The results and benefit that come back to you may be surprising.

(96) Jesus said, "The Kingdom of the Father is like a certain woman. She took a little leaven and concealed it in some dough, and made it into large loaves. Let him who has ears hear."

This parable is a variation of the mustard seed parable in saying #20. In the parables of Jesus we can usually identify what element we are dealing with by the gender of the person. A man generally represents our thinking side and a woman generally represents our emotional side. The Kingdom of the Father is a state of consciousness. This is the same state represented by the Kingdom of Heaven, the Christ Consciousness or the presence of God. Just as the ego is made larger by indulging in negative emotional states, so too does the spirit within grow as a result of love-based emotions. The leaven represents the love-based emotions, which in the beginning seem to be concealed within our normal emotions (concealed in some dough). But there is a quiet transformation which takes place. The more the spirit within grows, the more we tend to focus on the love-based emotions and the more peaceful we become. The process continues as the spirit grows large in comparison to the ego (large loaves).

(97) Jesus said, "The Kingdom of the Father is like a certain woman who was carrying a jar full of meal. While she was walking on a road, still some distance from home, the handle of the jar broke and the meal emptied out behind her on the road. She did not realize it; she had noticed no accident. When she reached her house, she set the jar down and found it empty. He who hath a mind to understand, let him understand."

This is a rare example of an "emptying out" parable. In order for us to grow spiritually and enter into the presence of God we must empty out the issues and emotional states which are taking the place of the presence of God within us. This is a gradual process. The unification of the inner self and the transformation of emotions accomplish their work in very small increments, to the point where the process continues on without the realization of exactly what is taking place. The peace, love and joy gradually build within us as we approach the point of awakening. When the awakening (enlightenment) takes place we are surprised by what has happened.

The ego fights back through the entire process until it has nothing more with which to fight. At that point the ego has no other choice than to recognize the awakened spirit within. This is the point described in the Gospel of John, Chapter 3, where John the Baptist admits he is not the Christ. The ego admits it is not the spirit within, and that it has to decrease in order for the spirit within to increase. The parable is about a woman, which indicates we are dealing with emotional issues. The jar represents the ego and the meal represents the issues and emotional states of the ego. The meal emptying out behind her on the road represents the gradual process of emptying out the issues and emotional states and leaving them behind (doing the spiritual exercises). When the woman reaches her house (the Kingdom of Heaven) she sets the jar down (the ego is set aside) and finds it empty (the ego has no remaining issues or negative emotional states with which to manipulate and control us).

The Kingdom of heaven is a state of consciousness which takes the place of our lower worldly thinking and feeling. The Kingdom is not added onto the things of the world but must replace them entirely. We must choose the Kingdom or the world; we cannot have both. This is why this parable is so important. It clearly demonstrates that what we have within us must be emptied out before we can enter into the Kingdom of Heaven.

> **(98) Jesus said, "The Kingdom of the Father is like a certain man who wanted to kill a powerful man. In his house he drew his sword and stuck it into the wall in order to find out whether his hand could carry through. Then he slew the powerful man."**

The parable is about a man, indicating that we are most interested in the mental or intellectual side. Spiritual growth requires a certain amount of courage, strength of character and persistence. A certain mind set is needed to do the exercises and see the process through to completion.

The powerful man represents the ego, which is the most powerful aspect of our mind before the spirit within is awakened. We must come to the realization, almost from the beginning of our spiritual journey, that the ego is the enemy. The ego and its issues and emotional states are the very things which stand between us and the presence of God in our lives. If we are to enter into the Kingdom, the ego must die.

What we really want to know is, "Can I actually do this? Can I really enter into the presence of God?" The answer can be demonstrated by beginning the exercises. The process starts with the observation of our thoughts and emotional reactions to things which happen in the world. Once we observe the ping-pong ball action between our thoughts and feelings as an emotional state is being built, we realize that the ego really is manipulating and controlling our life. We have caught the ego in the act. This is the first realization that the inner path is real.

As we continue on with the exercises we will have a spiritual experience where we get a small sample of the presence of God. This experience is confirmation that the process actually works. Once you have your first experience with the presence of God you will know that all of the Kingdom can be yours. This is what the man sticking his sword into the wall represents. When you have your first spiritual experience, you will know you have what it takes; you will know you can follow through. The process is the same. Persist and you will succeed. All the Father has will be given to you as you grow and mature in the presence of God.

(99) The disciples said to Him, "Your brothers and Your mother are standing outside." He said to them, "Those who do the will of My Father are My brothers and My mother. It is they who will enter the Kingdom of My Father."

We are all born with physical families. Once we seriously begin a spiritual journey, we also discover that we have a spiritual family. Unrelated by birth, we find that we are related and connected by consciousness and our relationship with God. Some people come to realize their entire life was in preparation for meeting a particular spiritual teacher and learning what he or she has to offer. On your spiritual journey you will find connections with others you couldn't have imagined before. Some call this a spiritual family which they believe re-incarnates as a group time after time.

Whatever your personal experience, you will find a connectedness not only with God but with others who share your spiritual journey. Many times you may remark about the strange coincidence which brought you and certain individuals together in your life. We live in an interactive universe where everything is connected through God. A coincidence is an incidence which is connected to another incidence, becoming co-incidences, related beyond our normal perception. You can think of the term coincidence as a condensed form of connected incidence. We are all connected through God; we just don't usually see the connection until we start perceiving the presence of God in everything. Then it all starts to become clear; there is only oneness.

(100) They showed Jesus a gold coin and said to Him, "Caesar's men demand taxes from us." He said to them, "Give Caesar what belongs to Caesar, give God what belongs to God, and give Me what is Mine."

The things of the world belong in the world. We all have physical needs relating to survival, health and comfort. These are things we require from the world. The ego has things it wants from the world as well. Empires require tribute and taxes to maintain armies and trade. When a country coins money, it institutes a system for its use. If we wish to make use of that system we need to comply with its conditions. Give Caesar what belongs to Caesar. This is why in similar sayings Jesus asked whose image was on the coin.

We also need to give God what belongs to God. We were given the spirit within, our personal source of life by God, out of the substance of God. We have an obligation to make that gift grow and prosper (the parable of the talents – saying #41). We also need to give a true spiritual teacher the attention and respect appropriate to his or her understanding of God and ability to guide others into the presence of God. This is what we need to give Jesus, the respect of an older brother on his spiritual path. We do that, not by worshiping him, but by listening closely to what he said and doing our best to understand what he is teaching us. We honor Jesus by doing the exercises, having the spiritual experiences, entering into the Kingdom, and becoming like him.

(101) Jesus said, "Whoever does not hate his father and mother as I do cannot become a disciple to Me. And whoever does not love his father and his mother as I do cannot become a disciple to Me. For My mother gave me falsehood, but My true Mother gave me life."

This is a more complete statement of saying #55. Family dynamics form, to a large degree, the issues and emotional traumas which determine the actions of the ego. Going through the process of self discovery uncovers those issues and demonstrates how the ego is manipulating and controlling us. With this understanding we can dismantle the ego by resolving the inner issues and traumas and unifying the inner self. One by one we are removing the tools the ego uses against us until there is nothing left. At this point the ego surrenders and releases its power and authority to the awakened spirit within. Our physical mothers do the best they can under the circumstances, but they are not prepared to give us the insights into the truth of God. This is something we must create within ourselves through the experience of living in the presence of God. It is the loving nature of God which the true mother represents. Truth comes to us as a result of changing our consciousness and entering into the presence of God.

(102) Jesus said, "Woe to the Pharisees, for they are like a dog sleeping in the manger of oxen, for neither does he eat nor does he let the oxen eat."

This is a parallel to saying #39. The outer forms of the mystery school system were controlled by the scribes and Pharisees, who had access to at least some, if not all, of the secret knowledge. The manger of oxen is the feeding trough where hay and grain were placed. A dog sleeping there does not eat hay or grain; neither will it allow the oxen to eat. So the Pharisees, having access to the secret knowledge, do not actually follow the practices or do any exercises, so they are not feeding their spirit within. Neither will they allow anyone who is interested in the knowledge to learn unless they are among the elite and are invited into the system. Everyone else is excluded from this crucial information. This has caused untold suffering among the common people who have a right to know the truth. It is the birthright of every human on the planet to know about the ego and the spirit, and how to awaken, raise and empower the spirit within. Each person will decide for himself what he wants to do, but we all deserve and need to have the information.

(103) Jesus said, "Fortunate is the man who knows where the brigands will enter, so that he may get up, muster his domain, and arm himself before they invade."

This is a parallel to part of saying #21. As we grow through the process of self discovery, we find that other people are not the only ones who will challenge us and try to get us to conform to the way we were. Our own ego will oppose our progress. It is necessary again for us to be on guard against the attacks which we know will come. Once we understand the ego and the tools and methods it uses against the growth of the spirit within, we can recognize where in our thoughts and feelings the ego will enter. We can then prepare ourselves and stop the damage which would result from the challenges to our new-found spirituality.

The spiritual experience of living in the presence of God is so important and transformational in our lives that we must do everything we can to keep the process alive and growing within us. Other people and our own ego will take this experience away from us if we allow them to do so. We must have the foresight, the courage and the inner strength to persist in the exercises and defend the awakening spirit within against all attacks until the spirit within has fully awakened and become empowered. This is the same principle as in saying #10 where Jesus is guarding the fire until it blazes. Once there, the power of the spirit within and the presence of God will stand on its own, like the city on a hill in saying #32, for all to see. The Kingdom of Heaven will be yours forever and nothing can take it away from you.

(104) They said to Jesus, "Come, let us pray today and let us fast." Jesus said "What is the sin I have committed, or wherein have I been defeated? But when the bridegroom leaves the bridal chamber, then let them fast and pray."

The bride, the bridegroom and the bridal chamber are symbols used to represent a specific aspect of the spiritual growth process. This process is referred to as the mystical marriage and represents the final entry into the Kingdom of Heaven and the presence of God. In the traditional mystery school system a student first learns the theology and basic intellectual principles of spirituality; then begins the actual practice of self discovery, inner transformation and unification of the inner self. This is the time requiring self discipline to keep with the practices and exercises so the inner process of transformation can become complete. This is the stage of the disciple, the disciplined one.

The end result of discipleship is the unification of the inner self, becoming one within: solitary, speaking with one voice. In the traditional mystery school system this is also known as becoming a "virgin" or attaining a state of purification of mind and heart. The "virgin" or purified state is required before the mystical marriage can take place. A man becomes the bridegroom with the bride representing God. A woman becomes the bride with God being the bridegroom. The mystical marriage is the unification with God, becoming one with God and all of creation. In John, Chapter 3 verse 2, Nicodemus recognizes the presence of God within Jesus, saying, "Rabbi, we know that you are a teacher come from God; for no one can do these signs that you do, unless God is with him." In John 3:29, "He who has the bride is the bridegroom". This is the mystical marriage, the unification of the individual with God, that 100% full conscious contact with God that is the Kingdom of Heaven, the Christ Consciousness.

If for some reason, after attaining the Christ Consciousness we should fall short (sin) or lose the experience of the Kingdom (be defeated) then we can fast (in regards to the world) and pray (return our attention back to God) to re-establish ourselves back into the Kingdom.

(105) Jesus said, "He who knows the father and the mother will be called the son of a harlot."

When we come to know the true nature of God, we can expect to receive a certain amount of disrespect from people who follow the outer form of religion. What we experience is a heresy to them. Keep in mind a heresy is simply a belief that is not within the doctrine of the church - outside the box.

We experience God in two basic forms represented by male and female: Father and Mother. The masculine form of the experience is revelation, a revealing of the inner knowledge, understanding and wisdom which is of God. The feminine form is the nurturing, supportive aspect of God which manifests as the unconditional love which comes from God. This is why some people refer to God as Mother / Father God. They are giving recognition to the two very different aspects of our experience of God.

(106) Jesus said, "When you make the two One, you will become the Sons of Man. And when you say, Mountain, move away, it will move away."

When we attain inner unification, having become one, we go through the mystical marriage and become one with God. Then we are a fully awakened and empowered spiritual being, a Son of Man. Then when we say, "Mountain, move away", it will move away. The mountain is an inner belief, usually having to do with authority figures. The spiritual process is the transfer of authority from the outside of us to the inside, from the world to God and the spirit within. It is also the unification of authority and responsibility within. When we combine authority and responsibility within, we gain control over our lives.

(107) Jesus said, "The kingdom is like a shepherd who had a hundred sheep. One of them, the largest, went astray. He left the ninety-nine and looked for that one until he found it. When he had gone to such trouble, he said, I care for you more than the ninety-nine."

The parable of the lost sheep is an important example of the difference between the inner and outer interpretations of the sayings of Jesus. The outer interpretation perceives the lost sheep as someone who has left the flock and has lost his way. Security comes from being part of the flock or congregation. As long as a person remains within the established doctrine he is safe. Leaving the established doctrine is not safe. One goes astray by not believing correctly. Many congregations perceive the role of the minister as being the shepherd: finding those who have gone astray and bringing them back to the flock.

The inner interpretation perceives the flock as a confined, limited belief system, thinking and believing inside of the box. The person who begins to think on his own begins to move out of the box, thus leaving the belief system of the congregation, or leaving the flock. In this example the sheep is the largest, which represents the strongest of the flock or congregation. This strength refers to strength of character and independence. It is this strength which not only enables the person to leave the congregation, but ultimately drives him to leave. This is the person seeking more than the established doctrine can provide. This is the person seeking true direct contact and connection with God. This is the beginning of a serious spiritual journey.

A strange and wonderful thing happens on this journey. In our search for God we not only find ourselves, but also we are found. The Kingdom is like the shepherd. Once we are seriously involved in our spiritual journey, the Kingdom comes and "finds" us. It is a cooperative process. In essence, it is our serious seeking which brings us to the attention of God in the first place. Once we are "found" we experience the unconditional love which comes from God. We feel loved more than the ninety-nine. God loves each of us equally, but as long as we remain inside the established doctrine, we are limited in our experience of God's love by our limited belief system. The Kingdom cannot be added onto the existing belief system with all of our issues and emotional traumas. We must resolve the issues and traumas to make room for the Kingdom. Resolving those issues and traumas brings us out of the flock, out of the ordinary consciousness of the world and into a condition where we can be identified as seriously seeking God. We are making room inside of us for the presence of God, creating a suitable home for the peace, love and joy which is of God. We were lost, and now are found.

(108) Jesus said, "He who will drink from My mouth will become like Me; I Myself shall become he, and the things that are hidden will be revealed to him."

"He who will drink from my mouth" is a person who understands what Jesus is saying. If we understand the principles and do the practices which Jesus is teaching, we will become like him. We will become a Christed being (I myself shall become he). It is not possible, nor is it necessary, to understand all of the things of God before we do the practices (exercises). We do not start out with an in-depth understanding, but a general intellectual concept of the teachings and where they are intended to lead us. That is what this author hopes to accomplish: to provide you with a general intellectual concept. The exercises themselves create the inner transformation required. As this inner transformation progresses, the presence of God and the associated spiritual experiences will bring the deeper understanding of the principles which we seek. The understanding comes from our direct experience with God (*gnosis*). The things which are hidden will all be revealed through the persistent practice of the exercises. Do the exercises, have the spiritual experiences, and then you will understand.

(109) Jesus said, "The kingdom is like a man who had a (hidden) treasure in his field without knowing it. And (after) he died, he left it to his son. The son did not know (about the treasure). He inherited the field and sold (it). And the one who bought it went plowing and found the treasure. He began to lend money at interest to whomever he wished."

The hidden treasure in the field is the sleeping spirit within (hidden within the field of consciousness). This is the normal state of people in the world: They have within them the living spirit, the substance of God, and they are unaware of it. We teach our children the things of the world and pass that legacy on to them, but because we didn't know about the nature and reality of the spirit within, our children receive only what we could leave them: the field of consciousness without knowing about the treasure of spirit and eternal life. Our children, too, will live their lives not knowing about the treasure within.

The one who goes plowing is the one who embarks on the journey of self-discovery and goes through the process of inner unification, plowing up the emotions and programming of the past. It is through this process that we discover the treasure of the spirit within. In the world, the one who is wealthy can lend money at interest to anyone. In spiritual terms, we have enough knowledge and understanding to teach others and share the wealth of wisdom which is of God. How much better would life be if we could learn about the spirit within and the contest between the spirit and the ego in our childhood? How would our lives and the lives of our children be transformed? If we only knew.

(110) Jesus said, "Whoever finds the world and becomes rich, let him renounce the world."

The world represents the ego. The ego is formed in response to the world and our need to interact with the world in which we find ourselves. The ego is a function of the body and the body is part of the world, so these terms are inter-related from the spiritual perspective. The ego sees the world as a place where it can gain wealth and power, and a number of people do just that. The problem is, they gain their wealth and power at the expense of the other people around them. The whole goal here is to give up or remove the ego: renounce the world (ego). Wealth and power are not the problem. The problem is the out-of-control egos which will do anything and hurt anyone to get what they want.

We have a responsibility to God and to each other. We do not live in this world alone. We are connected to one another, whether we like it or not. We cannot take from another or gain at another's expense without harming our spirit within. Once we begin to realize there are no separate actions, that everything is interconnected, and when we harm someone else we also harm ourselves, then we can begin to see how important it is to take control of our own ego and put a stop to its destructive behavior. In essence, to renounce the world is to put a stop to the insane and destructive behavior of our own ego.

(111) Jesus said, "The heavens and the earth will be rolled up in your presence; and the one who lives from the Living One will not see death." Does not Jesus say, "Whoever finds himself is superior to the world?"

When we go through the process of self-discovery and inner-unification, we can center our consciousness on the spirit within, thus connecting our consciousness with the part of us which has eternal life. From that point on, it does not matter what happens physically because who we are (our individuality) is maintained; we will not see death. The Living One is the living light of Spirit, God, who created us out of the substance of God which gives us our personal life, the spirit within. Finding our true self is the process of self-discovery and inner-unification which reveals and awakens the spirit within. The spirit within is superior to the ego (the world).

(112) Jesus said, "Woe to the flesh that depends on the soul; woe to the soul that depends on the flesh."

The body is dependant on the spirit, or soul, for its life. The spirit within is the source of our personal life, just as Spirit (God) is the source of all life everywhere. When we center our consciousness on the ego, we are making ourselves dependant on the body, which is a temporary creation. This is the equivalent of building our house on the sand; it will not last. The first death is the loss of our physical body. The second death is the loss of the consciousness attached to that body. The answer is to attach our consciousness to the spirit, which has eternal life. That way even when the temporary body is set aside, we retain our individuality and consciousness.

(113) His disciples said to Him, "When will the Kingdom come?" (Jesus said,) "It will not come by waiting for it. It will not be a matter of saying 'Here it is' or 'There it is.' Rather the Kingdom of the Father is spread out upon the earth, and men do not see it."

This is what people want to know; "When will the Kingdom come?" Some people believe it will come with the Second Coming of Christ. If they wait, it will come. Others believe they can enter the Kingdom by affirmation or decreeing themselves to be in the Kingdom. Jesus is saying none of these things will work. Rather, the Kingdom of the Father is spread out upon the earth, and men do not see it. If the Kingdom of the Father, or the Kingdom of Heaven, were a collective experience (happening to everyone at the same time) then Jesus is telling us it has already come (saying #51). The Kingdom is an individual experience, not a collective one. We enter into the Kingdom by our own efforts and dedication through the process of self-discovery and inner-unification. The Kingdom has been here all along, spread out upon the earth. The presence of God is in and of everything. It always has been; we just haven't perceived it. The Kingdom of the Father is a state of consciousness, not a place or a time. We enter into the Kingdom by changing our consciousness to coincide with the consciousness of God. It really is that simple.

(114) Simon Peter said to them, "Let Mary leave us, for women are not worthy of Life." Jesus said, "I Myself shall lead her in order to make her male, so that she too may become a living Spirit resembling you males. For every woman who will make herself Man will enter the Kingdom of Heaven."

In life we encounter many prejudices. People are prejudiced by gender, race, religion, ethnic origins, social position and many other conditions. The disciples were no exception. Women were considered more property than equals. Some branches of the mystery school system gave equal standing to women; some created relatively equal, but separate standing for women. Jesus did not see women as being inferior to men, but of equal value and importance to God.

The important thing Jesus is trying to get across is that it doesn't matter if a person is male or female; the balance between the masculine and feminine qualities within us is what is important. Balancing the masculine and the feminine also means balancing the intellectual and the emotional natures within us. We cannot sustain ourselves in the Kingdom if we are continually out of balance within ourselves. Part of what the journey of self discovery and inner unification produces is a balancing of all the qualities within. Everything joins in a seamless unity of balance and harmony. We come to peace with everything in our life and join in the oneness of God and all of creation. We become centered in Love and the presence of God, and act as a force for good and redemption in the world. As we fully and completely enter the Kingdom of Heaven, we become the mechanism through which God sends His Peace, Love and Joy into the world. Our thoughts, feelings and actions work together to bless all who come into our presence, and we are blessed in the process. Through us, the Kingdom of Heaven becomes a reality in the world.

THE EXERCISES

The Process of Self-Discovery

We live in a world of duality. The inner explanation of this is that there are two “selves” within us which we need to “discover”. The first self is the ego. This is the personality which develops during childhood and acts as our interface with the outer world. We gradually adopt the belief that we are the ego, and that is all there is within us. During the passage of life’s experiences, we come across hints and suggestions indicating that there is more to us than we have previously believed. This leads us to the discovery of the second “self” within, which is the spirit. This spirit is generally in a sleeping state, which makes it difficult to recognize.

We begin the process of self-discovery with the recognition of our dual nature: ego and spirit. Since the ego is well developed and is standing in the way of the spirit, we must come to recognize what the ego is doing and how it operates. With that understanding we can dismantle the ego and free ourselves from its tyranny. The ego operates just under the conscious level of the mind. When we identify ourselves with the ego and think that it is who we really are, the ego can operate without being noticed by the conscious mind. By expanding our awareness even slightly the actions and activity of the ego become apparent.

The ego follows the principle of divide and conquer. In keeping with that, the ego maintains a collection of issues and emotional traumas and perceived injuries. It is a type of laundry list from which the ego can pick and choose depending on the particular situation it faces. The purpose of the list of issues is not the event itself, but the emotional energy which can be generated by the issue. The ego derives its strength and energy from the emotions we experience. The types of energy the ego can use essentially as food come from the negative emotions which are fear- and pride-based. These include: fear, anger, hatred, guilt, envy, shame, lust, resentment, bitterness, superiority, prejudice, inferiority, disgust, revulsion and false pride. False pride is feeling that we are better than others. True pride is satisfaction in an accomplishment of a job well done. True pride remains internal; false pride is advertised to the rest of the world.

The spirit within also derives its energy from our emotions, but the nature of the energy itself is different. This difference can be expressed as a higher frequency, or a finer grain or consistency. This emotional energy is generated by the positive emotions of peace, love, joy, compassion, caring, happiness, gentleness, respect and true pride. The physical body is designed to produce the specific type of energy we request, based on the emotions we choose to experience, on a moment-by-moment basis. The ego manipulates us into experiencing almost exclusively negative-based emotions from which it derives its energy. The spirit cannot use the lower-based energy produced by the negative emotions, so it enters a type of hibernation, waiting for the proper type of emotional energy to become available. By manipulating us into the negative emotions, the ego has all the food it wants and at the same time is denying food to the spirit, which the ego sees as its primary competition. (The ego sees other egos as secondary competition.)

The ego uses a sequence of an initial trigger (internal or external), followed by an emotion related to the trigger, followed by a thought - usually a restatement of a conclusion we have come to about ourselves in the past. The thought acts as an internal trigger and the process continues to build one emotion on top of another until a strong emotional state is attained. This creates an energy banquet for the ego. The trigger can be external (an event: something someone says or does) or it can be internal (a thought). The emotions generated in this sequence are all related and based on the same issue so the end effect is a building of strength as one is added on to another, each reinforcing the others.

The first task in the discovery process is to look for the sequence: trigger, emotion, thought, emotion, thought, emotion, thought, as an emotional state is being built. It is not necessary to catch the sequence from the very beginning. Discovering the ego at any part of the sequence will work. In the early stages the emotional states come and go and we recognize that we have missed the entire thing hours or even days after the fact. Do not be discouraged; simply persist in looking for the sequence.

Observation

Observation is the practice of looking for patterns of thoughts, feelings or behaviors. Looking for the trigger, emotion, thought, emotion, thought sequence is the first skill in observation that we will work on. You will need some type of small notebook, something you can carry around with you wherever you go. In this notebook write three headings: **trigger, emotion** and **thought**. The trigger is usually an event, so you can also write **trigger (event)** to make the heading clearer. The goal is to write down what you observe in the trigger, emotion, thought, emotion, thought sequence. Don't be overly concerned about getting everything right in the beginning. If you can get one or two of the elements of the sequence, write them down. This will help you recognize more of the sequence as it happens again. It is not necessary to write down a long explanation of your thoughts. Write down just enough so you will have a clear idea of what the thought actually was.

A trigger (event) may be getting cut off in traffic, catching every red light, something someone says or does, the washing machine breaking down, being late for work - anything which triggers an emotional state or reaction. The event is usually remembered longer than the emotion, and the emotion is remembered longer than the thoughts. If all you remember is the event, write it down and leave the other categories blank. It's a start, and starting is very important. Remember, it doesn't have to be perfect; it just has to be done.

As you become more practiced at observation, you will catch the developing emotional state before it becomes full blown. One of the things you may experience is that the minute you recognize the developing emotional state, it stops. What has happened is the ego has been caught doing what it does, and like a child, does not like to be caught in the act. When this happens to you, you will know that what we are discussing about the ego really is true. The ego really does work to manipulate you and control your thoughts and emotions. At this point you have taken your first real step into a larger world of awareness.

With more practice, you will identify all three elements of a building emotional state: the trigger, the emotion involved, and a pattern of related thoughts. As you recognize what is going on, the building of the emotional state will stop. This initial success will also result in a complete failure at some point and you will experience a major emotional upset. What is happening is the ego, interrupted so many times, has become desperate for its emotional feeding. This failure to stop the emotional state is just part of the process and should not be taken seriously. It will show you that the process is going to take time and effort. You will come to know that you have a real fight on your hands. The ego is not just going to disappear. This is an inner war, and you are going to have to persist all the way through to the end. The process is simple; it's just not easy. Remember: every worthwhile project requires a great deal of work, and the greater the value, the greater the work. Continue observing until you have identified ten to twelve thoughts for each emotion identified.

What you will notice after a month or so of observation is that there are repetitive patterns in emotional states and related thoughts. Rewrite your list from the notebook so that all of the same or closely related emotions are grouped together. Create new headings based on the emotion (anger, guilt, frustration, etc.) and then list the associated thoughts under the related emotion. For most people the observations that were written down in the notebook will fall into three or four general categories based on emotions. These are the emotional states selected by the ego to generate its food. These are also the emotional states which are taking the place of the presence of God in your life. What you really need to realize at this point is this is exactly what the ego has to offer you for the rest of your life. Your list of emotions is your past. It will also be your future if you do not change your thoughts, emotions and actions today. So the question now becomes: Do you want these emotional states, or do you want the presence of God instead? This is where you have to make a choice. You can have these emotions, or you can have the deep abiding peace, the unconditional love which comes from God, and the joy of God in your life. You can't have both; you have to choose. If you choose the presence of God *all* of these negative emotions must go; nothing can remain. This may be the single most important decision of your life. Don't wait or put it off; decide now, once and for all.

The thoughts which are now organized by their related emotion represent the conclusions you have come to about yourself, or that have been programmed into your mind by others. This is a listing of the "self image" which is actually running your life. Now you can see what the ego is actually doing to you and why it has to go. The list of thoughts will act as a type of road map which you can use to identify where these thoughts and emotions came from in your past. There are three major sources for emotions and their related thoughts: traumas, programming and imprinting.

Traumas

Traumas are highly emotional events which happen to us in our life. Many of them happen during childhood, and our mind tries to make some sense of what has happened. Lacking the maturity of an adult, we, as children, cannot make proper associations of events in our lives. An example would be the divorce of our parents. The child often comes to the conclusion that he is somehow at fault for the break-up of the family. Sometimes a "bad" act of the child is selected by the child as the reason for the parents' actions. As adults, we clearly see that the actions of the child do not figure in to the actions of the parent. But the child does not have this level of perception, nor do they have the experience of the adult to guide them.

Dysfunctional families create multiple traumas in the child's life. Physical, emotional and mental abuses are taken very seriously by children. Denial is a common coping mechanism used to suppress the severity of the abuse, but the denial is just one more layer which has to be overcome during the self-discovery process. Denial has the effect of slowing down the process, forcing the individual to dig out hidden factors and events before effectively resolving them. The person who has developed a "laundry list" of what has been done to him (actual or perceived) has a head start in this regard. They know exactly what needs to be resolved.

These traumas have a specific internal structure to them. The structure is dual in nature, composed of an intellectual component and an emotional one. Each of the conclusions (thoughts) recorded on your list is strongly linked to the associated emotion. Each component (thought or emotion) has a memory of the other. We can use affirmations to alter the thought patterns, but if the emotions are left they will regenerate the thought patterns. We can also use emotional release techniques, but if the thoughts remain, they will regenerate the emotions. It may take six months to a year for the regeneration to take place, but it will happen. The answer is to resolve both the thoughts and the associated emotions together so nothing remains.

Issues

Each of the emotional states we experience fractures out into a group of issues. Each issue becomes a tool which the ego uses to manipulate us into the emotional state required to feed the ego. The ego hides these separate issues from our conscious view by constructing buffers around the issue. The buffer works to create a momentary disorientation as we move from our normal state of consciousness into the state associated with each particular issue and back again. The whole system flows together to the point where we rarely perceive anything has taken place. We become upset because that is how we handle the situation. It doesn't occur to us that anything else is happening. We just have issues with what is happening, how things are being done, or what is being said. We see ourselves as being in control of our lives, yet it is the ego which is controlling and manipulating us. We are the slave, not the master. The ego seeks to control everything except itself.

Each of these issues functions as a fractured piece of who we think we are, each born out of what happened to us, or what we perceive happened to us. The events don't have to be real; they only have to be perceived as real. Either way, the end result is the same. As you go through the process of self-discovery you will begin to see more clearly what the ego is doing and how it manipulates and controls your life. You will understand why the mystery school system portrays the ego as the one who opposes: Satan, or as the antichrist. The ego opposes the spirit within, corrupting our mind and heart and bringing unnecessary pain and suffering into our lives. Each issue is a launching pad for some form of suffering, experienced either by ourself, or by someone else. The hurtful things we do are born out of our own pain, and become the weapons of the ego.

Each issue can and must be resolved. By resolving an issue, we remove it from the arsenal the ego uses against us. In time, with enough work, we can resolve all of the issues the ego is using against us. With each issue resolved, we come one step closer to that 100% full conscious contact with God, one step closer to the Kingdom of Heaven and the Christ Consciousness. Once we are free of issues, we will see the world and all the creatures in it clearly. The world and our experience in it will have been completely transformed.

Programming

Much of the programming we impart to our children has a good and beneficial purpose. Don't talk to strangers, red means stop, green means go, look both ways before crossing the street, these are all examples of beneficial programming. Comments about the child repeated either to the child or within hearing distance become programmed into the child's mind. Sometimes the programming is not intentional, as illustrated in an old joke. Company was coming over and Mom took Johnny aside and told him he needed to be good for the evening. Johnny replied that he would be good for a quarter and mom said, "why can't you be good for nothing like your father?"

Programming also results in issues, but of a much less intense nature. The link between the emotional part and the thought part is weaker and easier to resolve. Programming can be harder to recognize because much of our belief system is based on things we consider to be "right" and most of that is the result of programming. The removal of the negative or limiting aspects of programming requires a re-examination of our entire belief system, keeping things which prove to be true and discarding those things which do not. This is a difficult process, for it requires us to question many cherished beliefs and attitudes. This is especially true when it comes to our beliefs about God. This is why the Gnostic approach is so important: There is no dogma or official doctrine to believe. When you do the exercises you will have the spiritual experiences. Those experiences will reveal the true nature of God to you, and will result in direct knowledge of God (gnosis).

Imprinting

Unintentional programming is imprinting. We are all subject to imprinting from parents, relatives, teachers, authority figures, friends, heroes and heroines, movie stars, and characters in movies, on television and in cartoons. We adopt patterns of speech, mannerisms, a look, a walk, an attitude through the process of imprinting.

Imprinting also produces issues which are generally weak and not easily recognized. Issues produced by imprinting are usually the last ones we find. The issues from traumas are big and generally more obvious. Our re-examination of our beliefs will reveal most, if not all, of the programming. Once those are resolved what remains is the result of imprinting. We must remain aware and continue to observe in order to uncover the imprinting. As we learn what our own voice is, it will be easier to recognize imprinting because the imprinting will appear in a different voice.

Recognizing the Different Voices Within

Each issue, whether from trauma, programming or imprinting, came from some exchange with someone. When that someone spoke to us, what they said becomes connected with the feelings we were experiencing at the time and a "voice" is created within us. When we go over the event in our mind a number of times, even if we are just asking ourselves "why did they do that", we are reinforcing what was said. We are, in effect, programming a new voice into our belief system. When there is nothing said and we are subjected only to an action or an attitude, we draw some sort of a conclusion about ourself or the other person (often both) and our conclusion becomes the new voice. Repeating the experience over and over in our mind reinforces the new voice and programs it into our belief system.

As we become more adept at observing our own thoughts and feelings, we will begin to recognize that some of the things we say are what our mother or father used to say. This is our first discovery of a different voice within us. This also marks our entry into a higher level of awareness. At this point we really don't know what our own voice is, but we can certainly recognize the obvious voices of relatives and authority figures in our lives. This gives us a place to start. With time and practice we will begin to discover voices from our own past, who we were at five or six years of age, who we were at fourteen or eighteen. Each stage of life produces a different voice which sounds like us but belongs in a different time and place. Each of these voices is not who we are now, and who we are now is not who we will become in the future.

There is one voice, which we do not recognize until much later in the process of self-discovery, which is our real voice: the voice of our own spirit. That voice sleeps, waiting to be awakened and empowered through the process of self-discovery and spiritual growth. That is the voice we will become as we stand in the presence of God and establish that 100% full conscious contact with God. Until then, our practice of observation continues, looking for the different voices within. Examine each thought and feeling and ask yourself, "Where did this come from? Is this the real me whom God created, or did this come from someone else?" Keep in mind that this is a constant process of refining, and in some circles it is referred to as the refiner's fire. All of the things which are not of God eventually will be burned away. Once you accept something as true does not mean it is true forever. It will be necessary to re-examine what we have accepted as true a number of times.

Gurdjieff[10] explained the process by stating that we were under 4,096 different laws, half of which were mandatory and half were voluntary. When we stop doing the voluntary ones, 2,048 laws remain. At that point half would be mandatory and half would be voluntary. When we stop following the voluntary ones, 1,024 remain. The process continues down through 512, 256, 128, 64, 32, 16, 8, 4, and 2, one of which is mandatory and one is voluntary. When we stop doing the last voluntary law only one law will remain. The final mandatory law is that we love one another. In the end, only the voice of God's love, which flows through us, will remain. That is our true voice.

The Process of Inner Unification

The fact that we are seriously interested in beginning a spiritual path means that the spirit within is stirring and becoming active. The spirit will become the guiding force in our process of inner unification. The ego is not interested in inner unification because that is where its control resides. As long as we remain divided, we remain conquered. The active spirit, by guiding us through the inner unification process, will free us from the ego's tyranny.

The process begins with the recognition of an issue. Each issue is connected to an emotion and a series of thoughts or conclusions we have adopted along the way. Some detective work is required on our part to connect the thoughts back to something in our past, real or perceived. Some time spent asking ourself "Where did this come from?" will usually produce some insights into the origin of the issue. Once the root cause of the issue is recognized, forgiveness and the transformation of the emotions are used to resolve the issue.

In resolving the issue we have taken that issue away from the ego. It is no longer available for energy generation, manipulation or control. By clearly recognizing an issue, we have broken down the buffer which the ego was using to protect its investment. This issue can never again be hidden from us. As we recognize more and more issues within, we become more and more aware of the ego and its activities. This increased level of awareness helps to awaken the spirit within, making it more active in our lives. The whole process becomes self-generating as the spirit within awakens.

One by one, issues are recognized, selected for resolution, resolved and removed from the consciousness. The issues which were standing in the place of the presence of God are gradually removed, and we begin to experience God's presence in our lives. With each resolved issue, a little more peace enters our life. We become less involved in the ego games people play. We gradually become passers-by, observing, learning, growing and increasing in knowledge and wisdom. We move out of the flock mentality and into individuality, making ourselves recognizable by the Spirit of God. It is only a matter of time before the shepherd finds us and we have a major spiritual experience. We will experience the intense love God has for us. From that point on, we will know for a certain fact what the true nature of God is. We will have acquired gnosis: direct knowledge of God. Believing will have become irrelevant.

Forgiveness and non-judgment

Forgiveness is the means of resolving the thoughts and conclusions associated with each issue. Each of these thoughts and conclusions were formed by a judgment about ourself, someone else or the world in which we live. The vast majority of these are negative in nature. Judgment can be defined as a condemning or negative conclusion about ourself, someone else or a condition in the world. When properly understood, forgiveness can be defined as the inner correction of a judgment. Forgiveness and non-judgment are designed to work hand-in-hand. It takes a great deal longer to correct a judgment through the process of forgiveness than it does to create a judgment and reinforce it in our consciousness. If we work on forgiveness and do not practice non-judgment, we will never come to a point of completion. We will continue to create more and more judgments which are in need of our forgiveness. Non-judgment, then, becomes an essential part of the process. If we can stop the formation of judgments, we will have a finite number of judgments to correct, and the forgiveness process will, at some point, become complete.

The key to non-judgment is to observe only. Become a passer-by. Observe without condemning. People do some very strange things. Sometimes it's a good trick to just observe and not condemn, but that is precisely what is required. You can observe that a person lies or steals or does a number of other things. It is appropriate to take protective action with such people, such as not trusting a person you know lies or steals. There is a profound difference between who and what a person is (a spiritual being, a child of God) and how he is behaving. We can still treat all people with respect, gentleness, and kindness without believing the lies they are trying to pass off on us. We still keep our doors locked and our property protected. We still see that people are held accountable for their actions against us and society. What we do not do is condemn them personally. People are held accountable for their behavior, nothing more, and nothing less.

We can forgive someone for what they have done to us and still hold them responsible for their actions. If this seems strange, we need to understand what forgiveness really does and why we need to practice forgiveness on a regular basis. Let's take a simple example of someone who is a neighbor and makes insulting or demeaning comments to you. When you object you are told it was meant to be funny; can't you take a joke? You feel hurt and are resentful about the way you are being treated. You try to make the person see that they are hurting you, but this only increases the abusive treatment you are receiving from them. You think, okay, I'll forgive them for what they have done to me; we will wipe the slate clean and start over with a fresh start. But nothing changes; the abusive behavior continues. You have to conclude that forgiveness doesn't work.

The key to understanding forgiveness is to realize that the intent is to stop the pain and suffering *you* are experiencing, not change the behavior of *other* people. You can limit your exposure to the abuse by not associating with the person involved. Do not attend functions where this behavior may be experienced. Avoid contact with the person. If confronted, tell him (or her) you do not care for his comments and behavior and do not want anything to do with him as long as this attitude and behavior continues. Don't argue; just walk away. In this way you are providing consequences to the other person (removing yourself as a target for his behavior). This is a form of holding him accountable for his actions.

Forgiveness does not make a person's behavior acceptable. So what exactly does forgiveness do? One of the reasons we are hurt by other people's words or behaviors is because it resonates with something inside of us, something which already hurts. People can "push our buttons" only because we have emotional issues which elicit specific responses. We may ask "Don't they know this hurts or bothers me?" Of course they do; that's why they are doing it. They are acting out of their own pain and causing pain in someone else is gratifying to them. Forgiveness is part of the process of resolving our inner issues so there is no emotional issue within us to resonate with the words or behaviors of other people. Once free of the inner emotional issues, the words of other people are just empty words, they have no meaning to us personally and we have no emotional stake in what is being said. In effect, we are unwiring the buttons other people are pushing. It's like a doorbell. When it rings, we answer the door. If we take the wire off of the button, the doorbell doesn't ring. The issues within us work the same way. When someone pushes one of our buttons, we answer. It's a conditioned response.

Forgiveness unwires the thought and conclusion part of the issue within, and when the emotional part is also unwired, someone pushing the button no longer elicits a reaction. That's how we know we have done our inner work. When someone does something or says something which has always caused a reaction, and we feel no reaction and the thoughts don't come, the issue is resolved. Each thought connected to an issue is either a type of conclusion we have come to, or it is something which has been programmed or imprinted into our consciousness.

We are dealing with things which have been repeated over and over again. What happens is, there is an internal reference system at work. When we hear or see something over and over again, each time we are exposed to it strengthens and reinforces the original. The subconscious mind recognizes the things for which there is an internal reference quickly. In effect the mind looks at everything which comes in and performs an instant analysis. The first question is, "Does this represent something dangerous?" The internal references are consulted, and if this internal reference says it is dangerous, then a protective reaction is generated. If the internal reference is deemed not dangerous, then the mind searches for what past actions were associated with this internal reference, and the same reaction is re-enacted. The logic is simple: I am still here, so whatever I did in the past must have worked, so do it again. Sometimes our behavior is inappropriate to the circumstances. For example we visit our parents and we find ourselves reacting like we were still children. We may be grown adults with our own children, but some of those old reactions are still there. Our subconscious mind and our ego don't care; this is the way the internal behavior reference is programmed and this is the way we are going to react now. A key in this comes from the word "reaction". We are re-acting, or acting again the way we did in the past. The same people, situation, words or actions elicit the same programmed reaction.

If we are going to change our reactions, we have to change the internal references. The difficulty we encounter is that the mind depends on these internal references to make sense of the world in which we live. In this process our mind tends to filter out anything which does not agree with an internal reference. So the changing of an internal reference does not happen by accident; it must be done intentionally. This is what an affirmation is designed to do: change the internal reference by repeating the new desired thought or conclusion over and over until it becomes the new internal reference. The way this works in the inner mind is that a new place is created for the new internal reference being programmed, and it exists right along side of the old reference. The old reference has been repeated thousands of times from repetitive actions of other people and the repetitive times we have gone over the same thing in our own mind. When the new reference builds up enough repetitive support to equal the old reference, the inner mind will bring the issue to the surface of our consciousness, in effect saying, "These two things are in conflict and they have the same number of inner references. Which one do you want to be the real reference?" This gives us the opportunity to select the new real inner reference. From that point on the new reference becomes the action of choice and the old pattern is no longer followed.

Forgiveness follows the same pattern, but if we can see where the old inner reference came from and realize it is a false conclusion, it greatly shortens the repetitive process of re-programming in the new reference. Realizing that our conclusion about something is wrong attaches a strong negative association with the old internal reference, lending strength and support to the new reference. We will still have some of the same old reactions, but we will usually quickly realize we are doing something which is now "wrong" and will move to correct it as soon as we can. The observation work of identifying the series of thoughts and conclusions associated with a particular emotion, and seeking where these thoughts and conclusions came from, leads us to the time, place and conditions of the early formation of the internal reference. Many times we can see that the thought or conclusion was the judgment we held as a child, without the maturity and experience we now have as an adult. It quickly becomes clear to us that the old thought or conclusion was wrong and needs to be corrected. This insight accelerates the re-programming process by identifying the old internal reference as "wrong", replacing it with a new "correct" reference.

So how does this work exactly? If one of your parents was an alcoholic and you were beaten as a child, how do you change that? You can't pretend it didn't happen. It's not the event itself that is important; it's our perception of ourself and our role in what happened that is staying with us. We may believe we were, or still are, bad, and that what happened was our fault.

("If I had been better, if I had done more, this wouldn't have happened.")

In some instances we were so young that we may need to ask some older family members about what went on in the past. Getting an adult understanding of our past family dynamics can shed a great deal of light on our perceptions. There may have been a serious injury which prevented the father from working, resulting in alcohol abuse and out-of-control anger. It may have been abuse by a family member in another generation which set the stage for what we experienced. The primary thing we must remember is that the child is generally not the problem. The adult is. The child is usually the available target for someone else's pain and anger. Realizing that we were not the cause of what happened, just an available target, helps remove us as a guilty party. We didn't deserve what happened. We were not bad or defective, we couldn't perform as an adult because we were a child; we were not responsible for what happened.

Once we realize an adult was responsible and not we as children, it is important to come to the realization that people perform very poorly in life. The hardest thing to grasp, however, is that people are doing the best they can under the circumstances. And yes, sometimes people's best is really bad. But the reality is if the individual in mind could actually have done better, they would have done so. Life is not risk free; bad things happen. The point is, what are we going to do about it now? The reality is, the person who did these things to us may no longer be alive, may not remember what he did, and more importantly may not care. The other person is not important; what we are experiencing (the pain and suffering) - that is what is important. The point of forgiveness is not to change the other person, but to stop the pain and suffering we are experiencing.

Realizing that we are not at fault is the first real step toward resolution. The next step is seeing that a bad thing happening to us is just another unfortunate aspect of life on planet earth. We can forgive the person involved for acting out of their own pain. Inside he may have been hurting more than we were. We cannot change him or his pain, but we sure can change the pain and suffering we experience. Forgiving the other person starts the process. Forgiving ourself for our condemning thoughts and conclusions breaks the connection to the past. Using affirmations after forgiveness can help re-establish a new perspective and a better self image.

Every thought and conclusion needs to be examined and re-evaluated based on our mature adult understanding and wisdom. As we go through our belief system one item at a time, we can gradually correct the thoughts and conclusions we made as a child which are still running our life. You will find forgiving someone else is easier than forgiving yourself. Start with forgiving others first so you get used to the process. Then focus your work on forgiving yourself. You will discover that 90% of the work of forgiveness is forgiving yourself. You must forgive yourself for all of the things you have done, and all of the things you believe you should have done but failed to do. Remember in the end, the judgment you give will be the judgment you receive. When you have forgiven everything, you are truly forgiven. When you are free of judging anything, you are free of being judged.

The Forgiveness Exercise

A forgiveness exercise should be done in a place where it is quiet and where you will not be disturbed for about 20 minutes. Close your eyes and take several deep breaths and slowly let them out to help you relax. Select an event from your past. As you remember the event, imagine yourself as an observer of the event, not a participant. You can stop the event at any point. Observe yourself as the child you were when the event happened. When you stop the event, go and talk to the child and explain what happened from an adult perspective. Tell the child he is not at fault; he (or she) did nothing wrong. If some behavior of the child was wrong, tell the child this is a learning experience and he will not do this again in the future. Explain to the child that adults often over-react to situations and this does not mean the child is bad, defective or anything else which may have been said to the child during the event. Hug the child and reassure him he is safe and he is loved.

If you find interacting with the child too difficult, imagine an angel appearing and doing these things for you. The purpose is to re-program the event in your own mind so you have a new set of thoughts and conclusions about yourself. The event has not changed, but your inner experience of the event has. If you can manage it, become the child and tell the adult that you forgive him. As the child, hug the adult and tell him that you love him. If you cannot, have the angel do it for you.

If the emotions are too painful for you to do the exercise, try moving the event further away, reducing its intensity by distance or try seeing it in black and white rather than color. You can also imagine it on a screen, as if it were a movie or on television. Anything that reduces the intensity to the point where you can do the exercise will help.

What if you can't remember the actual event? The actual event and the actual details are not as important as how you perceived the event. Your reconstruction of the event only needs to represent what you perceived. You can make up an event that represents the actual event as you perceived it. The inner mind does not know the difference between what we think is reality and what actually occurred. We are really dealing with our memories and perceptions, anyway.

Sometimes when forgiving an adult in these exercises the adult will stiffen up and resist the forgiveness or being hugged. It's okay, just let it play out in your mind. This is something which will need to be repeated a number of times. The exercise may change as it is repeated. You may get different insights into the workings of your own mind or something totally unexpected may happen. Let the exercise play out and observe what is happening.

After a number of repeated exercises on the same event, you may feel it is time to move on to another event. The nature of the inner mind is that it takes time to make the needed changes. You can think of these changes taking place in layers, like the layers of an onion. Each series of forgiveness exercises resolves a layer, and when you go on to another event keep in mind that you will return to this issue again in the future to resolve another layer. Eventually you will discover that one or more of your issues simply do not come up any more, even when someone is pushing your buttons to get you going again. When there is no internal reaction and you can remain peaceful and focused on the present rather than being dragged into the past, the issue is resolved. The number of layers depends on how many times and how many different ways this issue has been reinforced. The greater the repetition and the greater the variety of ways this issue has been experienced, the more layers there will be.

The time it takes to resolve an issue varies greatly from one individual to the next. It takes as long as it takes. There is no fixed time. The one thing you can be certain of is that if you persist, you will succeed. The second half of the forgiveness exercise deals with the emotions.

The Transformation of Emotions

In order to work with emotions we need to look at them differently. Emotions are not like the thoughts we have. Emotions are a form of energy which is why they can act as food for either the ego or the spirit. We can think of an emotion like water and ice. Water flows, ice does not; ice remains where it is. What happens when we stop feeling an emotion? If it is energy, it can't disappear; it has to change form. This is exactly what happens. When we stop experiencing an emotion it changes form, like water turning into ice. The emotion solidifies and resides within our body. Anger resides in the liver, bitterness in the pancreas, resentment in the spleen. When we activate an emotion it changes state again becoming fluid, flowing through us like water in a river. When we stop experiencing the emotion, it solidifies.

We can use this quality to our advantage. The solid form cannot be changed, but the fluid form can. While we are feeling an emotion, we can change the nature of the emotion into anything we choose. We do this all the time in the outer world. We turn on a switch and electricity flows through a light bulb. The electricity changes to heat, and the heat changes to light. The emotional form of energy our body produces is no different. We can change the nature or form of the emotional energy while it is flowing. We may think our emotions are not under our control, but they are. We can use our thoughts to guide our emotions.

Here is how the second half of a forgiveness exercise works. Once you have corrected the thoughts involved with an event, relax again with several deep breaths. Start feeling the emotion involved in the event you are working with. Start small. The idea here is that we are dealing with something very large and strong. It is like emptying a swimming pool, but rather than trying to do it all at the same time, we are going to empty the pool one cup of water at a time. Yes, it's going to take a long time, but anyone can move a cup of water. We are going to employ the same tactic with emotions. Large amounts of emotional energy are overwhelming; small amounts can be handled, and most importantly, easily transformed into another emotion.

If anger is the emotion you are working with, feel a small amount of anger. Just enough so you know it is anger and not enough where it is taking over. It will help if you will visualize holding the small amount of anger in your hands, as if you had captured a butterfly. Begin on one side of your body and physically move your hands slowly over to the other side. While you are doing this, change the emotion you are experiencing over to love. In the beginning, and especially with strong emotions, it will be very difficult to get to love. Don't be overly concerned. Just move the emotion as far as you can. There is a point in the middle, the point of neutrality, where the emotion seems to lose its character. During each exercise we want to move the emotion more and more into love, past the point of neutrality. Negative emotions used by the ego are all on the same side of the point of neutrality. The love-based emotions used by the spirit are on the other side of the point of neutrality. Piece-by-piece we want to move all of the negative emotions across the point of neutrality and into the love-based emotions.

As you conclude the exercise and stop feeling the emotion, it solidifies in the form in which it was last experienced. The anger experienced has been transformed into love and stored as love in the body. The anger transformed no longer exists as anger, only as love. The emotional energy is still there, but its form has changed. As you do the forgiveness exercises the thoughts and attitudes to the people in your life will start to change. You will see them in a different light and your feelings toward them will also change. As your thoughts and feelings toward them change, your relationship with them will also change. Some will move closer to you, and others will move further away. Your life will change and so will your relationships. Your real spiritual journey of transformation has begun.

The forgiveness exercise will have to be repeated a number of times. With practice a complete forgiveness exercise will take only 2 to 3 minutes. You can repeat the exercise or do a series of exercises during your 20-minute exercise period. Do not do the transformation of emotion exercises back-to-back. Do the thought re-programming exercise in between. Work the exercises in pairs: thought re-programming, and then emotional transformation. Don't be too surprised if you begin feeling tired after the exercises. The inner work of transformation can be very draining. Because of this you should not do this work for long periods of time. Three sessions of 20 minutes each, spread out over a day's time, is a serious spiritual path.

Resolving Inner Traumas

The events which have traumatized us are the strongest emotionally, and will take the most time and effort to resolve. The two-part forgiveness exercise described above can resolve most traumatic events but is not a substitute for professional psychiatric or psychological treatment or counseling. Beginning a spiritual path requires a relatively normally functioning person. The conditions described are considered to be within the range of normal behavior and common experiences.

Traumatic events can be a physically, emotionally or verbally abusive parent or close relative, the divorce or death of one or more parents or siblings, neglect or abandonment, or a number of similar occurrences. The resulting emotional states can be anger, guilt, fear, shame, resentment, bitterness or envy. Depression is often an element in the emotional mix, and like the other emotions, may come and go. We have a tendency to excuse our emotional states and experiences because they really are a somewhat normal part of the life experience. As "normal" as these experiences may be, the resulting thought patterns and emotional states are taking the place of the Kingdom of God within us. From a spiritual perspective, that really is the bottom line. All of the things we have been through are the normal experiences of the world. We can have our life filled with those experiences or we can choose to remove those thoughts and emotions from our life and replace them with the presence of God.

Sometimes we will have a really bad dream, and the memory of that dream stays with us for a very long time. Compare that to an ordinary dream. With the ordinary dream we can't remember what the dream was once we have gone on to other thoughts in the course of our day. The difference is the emotional content. The stronger the emotional content of the dream the longer we remember the dream. Traumatic events are the same way: the stronger the emotional content of the event, the longer it stays with us and the more disturbing it becomes in our life. The forgiveness exercise with the transformation of the emotions gradually reduces and eventually eliminates the emotional content of the traumatic event. As that happens, the intensity of the experience fades and eventually becomes a distant memory. Yes, if the subject comes up in discussion, we can remember what happened to us, but lacking the emotional content, it no longer is a factor in our life. We have become free of the past.

Resolving Inner Issues

The remaining inner issues from programming and imprinting have significantly lower levels of emotional content, and as a result more often play a minor role in our lives. The process for resolving them is the same: re-program the thought patterns based on our mature adult perspective and transform the emotional content into love-based emotions. The main difference is that we must be more observant because the programming and imprinting is much more subtle than the traumas in our life. Observation must be a constant practice in our life if we are going to complete our spiritual journey.

When I was a child, my mother liked birds and chased cats away to protect the birds. If a cat showed up we were told not to feed it or give it a name. By ignoring the cat it would go away. Several years ago a cat came to our back door and began to meow. We had seen this cat before in the area and assumed it to be a wild cat. It was the 4th of December, 2000, with snow and cold weather. We opened the door to see if the cat would come into the house, which it did. I said what had been imprinted in my mind as a child, "We are not feeding it or giving it a name." My wife recognized the cat was starving and cold, and said, "I'm naming it 'Shadow'. Here Shadow, would you like some food?" All we had was some canned dog food. When I saw the cat eating dog food as fast as it could gobble it down, it broke my heart. I realized that what I said was not me, but my mother speaking through the process of imprinting.

The cat not only gained a home, but I was able to remove one of the few remaining blocks to the full presence of God in my life. The amount of love flowing from God into my life increased dramatically. It became a transformational moment in my life and I give thanks to God for sending me a cat. We tend to think the major events and decisions in our lives are the most defining. Once we go through the process of self-discovery and inner-unification, we begin to see the small everyday decisions and experiences form the backbone and structure of our life. The things we do and feel everyday determine how we handle the major events in our lives, not the other way around. This is why the everyday practice of forgiveness is so transformational in our lives. Piece-by-piece we transform our thoughts and feelings, each step almost insignificant on its own, but the end result is profound and completely life-changing. Step-by-step we enter the Kingdom of God, changing our consciousness, our awareness, and our life experience from the ordinary into the extraordinary.

The inner experience of gnosis demonstrates to us that Jesus was an ordinary person having an extraordinary experience. That perspective becomes very clear to us as we, too, begin having the insights and experiences that come with the presence of God in our lives. As our life is transformed by the flowing of God's love through us, we begin to see the teachings of Jesus in a more personal and intimate way. It's not a matter of just understanding the teachings of Jesus. In the end we experience his teachings personally. We understand them because we are living them. Jesus said, "follow me" and we have. The Kingdom of Heaven is within, and we have entered, becoming one with God and all of creation.

Becoming Your True Self

When we have grown up functioning from the ego we really do not understand or perceive what we would be like if the ego were gone. We may think we might just disappear, but that is the ego leading us into not doing our spiritual growth. For a moment, imagine what it would be like to be totally at peace, totally connected to God and all of creation. Imagine what it would be like to have an unlimited amount of pure love flowing through you out into the world, touching the lives of people around you. While that is sinking in, imagine what it would be like to have direct knowledge of God, knowing God as you know your best friend, being able to converse directly with God in your mind, as you would with someone very close to you. Imagine how you would feel. Can you imagine yourself going through your day not feeling hassled or angry or guilty about anything? Can you imagine taking on life's challenges peacefully and lovingly, being gently guided by God in everything that you do?

If you can imagine these things you have just seen in your mind's eye what your true self can be. This is not an overnight process. It will take a number of years to accomplish this vision you have of your true self. The years are going to pass one way or another. The question is, when these years have passed, do you want to be like you are now, or like you have just imagined? Nothing is cast in concrete. The future is yours to choose. The path of spiritual growth described in the teachings of Jesus can bring you into the Kingdom of Heaven - into the full presence of God and into His peace, love and joy. It's a system that has been working for 2,000 years, and it will work for you.

Functioning From Love

The forgiveness exercises are designed to gradually remove the things that are blocking your awareness of the presence of God in your life. As the spirit awakens it will need to be fed with the love-based emotions to help it grow and mature. Positive thinking has done a lot to help change people's lives. It's time to take the next step into positive feeling. By focusing our thoughts on peaceful, loving things, we are telling our body to produce the loving feelings the spirit within needs to grow and develop. Through love the spirit within becomes empowered. By concentrating on radiating love from ourselves out to others in this world, we are helping to create the flow of love which comes from God. The love which then comes from God and flows through us out into the world blesses us, brings us closer to God, and unfolds the true self within. Through focusing on love-based emotions that we align ourselves with the consciousness of God, raising our awareness, increasing our connectedness, and finally become one with God.

The more we practice loving thoughts and loving feelings, the easier and more automatic the whole process becomes. As we practice gentleness and kindness with others we soften the hardness we have learned from the world. We become more caring and involved in life. We begin the process of making a difference, not only in our own life, but in the lives of other people around us. As we bless the lives of others, God blesses our life in return. Functioning from love takes lots of practice. The good news is we have hundreds, if not thousands, of chances to practice functioning from love every day. Every interaction with another person, an animal or a plant is an opportunity for us to function from love. The more we function from love the closer we become to God, and the more connected we become to God and all of creation. It is a gradual process; don't wait for the perfect time to start. The perfect time is now, the perfect place is here.

Recognizing the Christ

One practice which can help the growing spirit within is to imagine each person you encounter as Christ. Sometimes it is hard to do because of another's behavior or attitude, but try to imagine that Christ is there, asleep inside of them. Treat each and every person with the deep respect you would have for Christ if He were standing there instead. Make it a practice to imagine that you see Christ in everyone. Imagine Christ in the people you see walking down the street, or in the grocery store. Imagine each child you see as a young Christ with his whole life ahead of him. Imagine the possibilities these young people have as they grow up with the spirit of Christ within them.

As you practice seeing the Christ in each and every person, the whole concept of the spirit within will become more and more real to you. You will come to the point where you really do see the Christ in other people. Then the day will come when you look in the mirror and see the Christ in you. This is the whole point of the exercise: to get you to actually see the Christ in you. You are God's beloved child, and you were created to become a Christed being. God is waiting for you to see who and what you really are. The time has come for Christ to be born - in you!

[1] Out of Egypt, Ahmed Osman, Century – London, 1998, Pg 245.

[2] Out of Egypt, Ahmed Osman, Century – London, 1998, Pg 244.

[3] The Gospel of Thomas Annotated & Explained, Stevan Davies, Skylight Paths Publishing, 2002. Pg 71.

[4] The Gospel of Thomas – Unearthing the Lost Words of Jesus, Dart & Riegert, Ulysses Press, 1998. Pg 44.

[5] The Gospel of Thomas Annotated & Explained, Stevan Davies, Skylight Paths Publishing, 2002. Pg 77.

[6] The Gospel of Thomas – Unearthing the Lost Words of Jesus, Dart & Riegert, Ulysses Press, 1998. Pg 46.

[7] Gospel of Thomas Annotated & Explained, Stevan Davies, Skylight Paths Publishing, 2002. Pg 79.

[8] Gospel of Thomas Annotated & Explained, Stevan Davies, Skylight Paths Publishing, 2002. Pg 104.

[9] Jonathan Livingston Seagull, Richard Bach, Avon, 1973, Pg. 81.

[10] Gurdjieff & Ouspensky, Maurice Nicoll, Shambhala, 1984.